ANGEL OF THE JUDGMENT

# Angel

# of the Judgment

## a life of
## Vincent Ferrer

by S. M. C.

Ave Maria Press
Notre Dame, Indiana

NIHIL OBSTAT
Thomas E. Bird, S.T.D.

IMPRIMATUR
✠ Joseph
Archiepiscopus Birminghamiensis

Birminghamiae die 1 a Septembris 1953

Library of Congress Catalog Card Number: 54-5298

Manufactured in the United States of America

# FOREWORD

There is no lengthy bibliography to be appended to this book, because practically all the material was obtained from Père Fages' *Histoire de Saint Vincent Ferrier* which is such a rich storehouse that the only difficulty lies in making a selection. I wish to offer my most grateful thanks to the Father Prior of the Dominicans of Paris for his kind permission to use this material as far as I choose.

For the rest, Mother Prioress of the Dominican Priory at Stone very kindly lent me an edition of the sermons of Saint Vincent. This edition is mentioned by Père Fages. *La meilleure edition des sermons de Saint Vincent Ferrier est sans contredit celle qui fut publiée a Valence, en 1694, par les soins des religieux du couvent, avec des extraits du manuscrit autographe.* And these sufficed to fill in the remainder of the picture.

*S.M.C.*

# CONTENTS

part **I**

# The Man

# Chapter I

## *An Apostle*

The whole countryside was in a ferment.

From early dawn travellers had been pouring into the little Spanish town with its narrow streets and houses of wood or sunbaked clay, houses whose upper storeys overhung the road. Just beyond the town stood the priory of the Friars Preachers adjoining its large and beautiful church. The streets of the place itself met in the market square where, for three days now, workmen had been busy erecting a platform raised ten feet above the ground. Only that morning they had brought out a portable wooden altar and a carved wooden pulpit.

The magistrates, town council—call them what you will —who administered the affairs of the place and its surrounding countryside, had been driven to neglect their ordinary avocations, for there was so much else to do. All the town's best tapestries and hangings had to be brought out from store; every barn and outhouse in the place had to be requisitioned and cleared; holes had to be dug in the ground and fires built ready to cook quantities of food

3

which had been taken from every shop and store, brought in from all the neighboring farms. The caterers were not, however, unduly anxious about having a sufficiency, for they had heard of more than one instance of food multiplied, and never had their expected guests, nor their hosts either, been known to go short.

All through the morning, peasants from the surrounding country poured in, whole families, men, women and children. Towards noon, these began to give place to wealthier folk, landowners and professional men. Never, even on fair days, had the inhabitants seen such a concourse of people, pushing, jostling, struggling for places in the deep files which were forming up either side of the road.

Sometimes one would pass along leading a blind man, helping a lame woman, pushing the wheeled chair of a cripple, carrying a sick child. Then the crowd would move aside to give the newcomers place in the forefront of the tightly packed ranks.

Up and down the road the village dignitaries were patrolling, exhorting the masses of people to keep the way clear, pausing every now and then to look down the dusty road, wrinkling up eyes palmshaded from the glare.

From time to time breathless messengers would announce:

"He is leaving his last halting-place."

"His followers are forming up."

"He has started and is now on his way."

Then a roar came from the waiting crowd: "He is coming! Look, he is coming." The massed folk on the roadside swayed and surged, standing tiptoe to look over each other's shoulders along the eastern road. Now, far down the path stretching between sun-parched fields could be seen a tiny rolling cloud of dust.

4

The dust cloud rolled steadily nearer, grew larger and larger, and at the core of it could be seen a vast solid black mass, thousands, literally thousands of people, marching forward shoulder to shoulder. Then, above the myriad indeterminate noises of a waiting crowd could be heard the chanting, a great diapason note, of the huge concourse.

*"Miserere mei, Deus, secundum magnam misericordiam tuam."*

Down the road they came, and the watchers by the wayside could distinguish forms and faces: first a great company of women, then an even larger company of men, all marshalled by friars, monks, or secular priests walking on the outskirts. These were followed by a picked choir of men several hundred strong. Mingling with the chant could be heard a sound as of heavily falling rain. Taken by surprise, the waiting crowd involuntarily glanced up at the iron-blue ceiling of the heavens. But it was not an oncoming thunderstorm, it was the band of flagellants, expiating their own sins or those of the world, pleading for mercy, or love-sick with the burning flame of Crucified Love.

Then came two lines of men walking three or four abreast, carrying a barrier of staves and lining the roadside, a guard, not so much of honor, as for the protection of the man riding the little she-ass in the center of the road. He was an old man, an ugly man judged by ordinary standards, as weathered as a twisted moorland oak; for his nose was long and his cheek bones almost seemed to cut through the skin of his face, parchment-colored through exposure to sun and wind; save for the ring of his tonsure his head was bald. He was dressed in a coarse white habit and a disreputable old brown-black cappa, and the trappings of his sorry steed, a makeshift saddle and the stirrups' wooden blocks suspended by cord, were shabby enough to disgrace a beggar.

In his right hand he held a large wooden cross. His eyes were the only striking thing about this man, for they were large, very dark and full of fire, holding in their depths an extraordinary impression of youthfulness. But to the crowds round him, the man was something colossal, touched with the reflected splendor of the Divinity, more than human in love and pity, terrible in righteous wrath. As soon as they glimpsed him, they surged forward shouting:

"Master Vincent! Master Vincent!" And the guard was obliged to use force to hold them back, interposing the staves held from one to the other, lest in their excitement they should press so hard on the frail old man as to crush him to death. Suddenly the pushing, trampling mass of people parted and a procession of sick folk made their way to the forefront. A woman holding a dying child ran to the barrier:

"Fray Vincent! Fray Vincent! My baby, my first born."

The luminous eyes of the old man turned smiling on the suppliant. The cross was raised in blessing. The baby stretching out its little arms laughed in its mother's face.

Now a cripple drags himself up, calling for help; and as the cross is again raised in blessing, he flings away his crutches and begins to dance with joy.

A blind girl, who has crept through the pitying guards to touch the friar's habit, is shouting:

"I can see! I can see!" And the people are shouting and cheering, half-beside themselves with joy.

Suddenly, someone notices that the miracle-worker is no longer there. He has taken advantage of the excitement to

6

slip away to the priory of his own Order, there on the outskirts of the town, where his brethren are waiting to let
him in.

The prior in the porch receives him with respect, and
after asking for his blessing, Father Vincent slips quietly
to the church to kneel there in prayer, while the community, divided between pleasure and anxiety, is begging
the intercession of the saints to prevent the excited mob
outside from tearing down doors and windows, in their
frenzy to catch another glimpse of the miracle-worker.

Those in charge of Friar Vincent's cortège are used to
such scenes. So, tactfully, by pointing out the physical needs
of the great band which has invaded the town, they turn
all thoughts in the direction of hospitality. There are four
or five thousand to be fed and settled for the night, especially the womenfolk among them, for Master Vincent is
most particular that these should be suitably cared for
and lodged.

Meanwhile the friar has gone to the cell prepared for
him. He is not in the enclosure, for that would jeopardize the
privacy of the community, but in the guest quarters where
the town officials and others who have come, sometimes
from a great distance, to consult him, may have easy ac-
cess. And there he sits, receiving visitor after visitor without thought for himself or his own weariness, showing each
one the same unfailing courtesy and kindly attention until
the night is far advanced and the last visitor has left him.

At last he is alone and free to open the packages he
always carries with him, and which have been brought into
his cell. Taking out ink-horn, quill, bundles of manuscripts,
and fresh sheets of vellum, he begins to read and write,
preparing his sermon for next day.

The friar who has been charged with the care of the

visitor, moved by pious curiosity, has made himself a peephole in one of the door panels, and from this coign of vantage he watches him. Hour after hour Friar Vincent works on, reading, writing, annotating; does he never sleep?

At times he prays aloud:

*From* The Treaty of the Spiritual Life.

"O good Jesus, grant that I may love You from the inmost depths of my heart, that I may have an abiding fear of You, that I may adore You; that I may be filled with a burning zeal for Your honor, a zeal which will shrink at nothing. Grant that Your glory may be my only thought, and that I may have the greatest horror of every outrage offered to You; above all what You have suffered from me, through me, or by reason of me.

"Give me the grace to know You as my adorable Lord, I who am Your poor and humble creature; to return constant thanks for all Your benefits from a heart which is overflowing with gratitude. Grant that in everything I may bless, praise and glorify You with the joy of an overflowing heart. Grant that I may be ready to obey You, to submit myself to You in all things, that so I may experience, as a lifegiving savor, Your most sweet and ineffable goodness, sharing in Your divine bounty in the company of Your angels and apostles, unworthy and ungrateful as I am."

At last the watcher sees him, quite worn out, rest his arms on the table and pillow his head upon them to snatch an hour or two of uneasy sleep. With dawn he is up again, and having said Prime with the community, he begins to prepare for Mass.

Meanwhile, throughout the night the crowd has been gathering, thousands of them, for their number has been augmented by night travellers until there cannot now be fewer than twelve thousand, packing the square, lining every wall, every window-ledge, even the roofs of the surrounding houses. The choir is massed under the platform, and everywhere priests, friars, monks are moving, marshalling, exhorting and answering the numberless questions put to them.

Now it is the hour for Mass, and Friar Vincent, vested, appears at the foot of the altar on the platform. What a change! The people stare and stare again; how could they ever have fancied him old? He is young with a voice like a silver trumpet, strong, liquid and musical. Look at the spaciousness of his gestures; his outflung arms seem to embrace the world.

The choir, most carefully picked and trained, sings the Mass for the day, and the whole ritual weaves itself magnificently round the unique, the infinite act of Sacrifice. At its conclusion, Friar Vincent in his habit and cappa mounts the pulpit:

"*Et nunc dixi vobis priusquam fiat.* These words are taken from the fourteenth chapter of the holy Gospel according to Saint John. Let us say the *Hail Mary\** that the grace of God may be in my words and that what I am going to say may serve to the salvation of souls. *From a sermon on Antichrist.*

"Antichrist will subjugate the world in four ways. First, like a fisherman throwing his net, he will try to capture souls by a show of riches, by offering honors, by appealing to their greed and sensuality. The Wise Man says: *Man knoweth not his own end;* but as fishes are taken by the hook, and as birds are caught with the snare, so men are taken in the evil time, when it shall suddenly come upon

---

\* S. Vincent Ferrer was the first to introduce the *Ave* at the beginning of sermons.

them. And Saint John says: *Love not the world nor the things that are in the world.*

"Again Antichrist will direct his attacks against simple folk who, because their hearts are turned to Him in rectitude of intention, are so pleasing to God. He will make use of magic, and produce lifelike apparitions, which are, after all, the merest trickery. He will bring down fire from heaven, and make images speak, for the demon can cause their lips to move. To all appearance, he will recall the dead spirit of your father, and phantom infants will seem to speak.

"Those in the third category whom he will try to seduce are learned folk, such as masters and doctors of civil and canon law, who can argue and grasp proofs of things. Against these Antichrist will weave spells of enchantment, bringing out the most subtle arguments, the most seductive reasoning, to render these learned men tongue-tied and incapable of answering. It is not difficult to understand how this is done since the demon already holds their souls in the chains of sin; for the greater their knowledge the more heavily burdened will be their consciences if they do not live up to it. If he can hold their souls in chains it is easy for him to bind a morsel of flesh like the tongue so that they cannot speak except what he chooses.

"The remedy for this state of bondage is faith, which follows simple obedience and not argument or reasoning. Argument may be good for the strengthening of the intelligence, but it is not the true foundation of faith. Those whose faith rests on reason will lose it when they hear the specious reasoning of Antichrist. Those on the contrary who rely on a firm belief founded on obedience will reply: 'Away with your arguments! Such reasonings are not the grounds of *my* faith.'

10

"Saint Ambrose says: *Leave argument aside in matters of faith.* And Saint Paul to the Corinthians: *That your faith might not stand on the wisdom of men but on the power of God.* The virtue that Christ loved best was obedience. *Et nunc dixi vobis priusquam fiat.* Listen now, brethren, for this concerns you closely.

"The fourth condition of persons to be tempted are the saints and the perfect who lead a holy life in the contemplation of the secrets of God; though in body they are still in this world, they can more truly be said to be in that to come. As Saint Paul says: *Our conversation is in heaven.* Towards such Antichrist will show himself a pitiless tyrant, striving by sufferings of all kinds to force them against their wills to obey him. Then no Christian will be able to purchase even the necessities of life, save at the cost of denying Christ. The Blessed Sacrament must be taken down from the altars and the sacred vessels and linen and the images of the saints must be burnt, and Christians will be driven to hide in the deserts, eating grass for their food. Daniel has predicted this: *And he shall speak words against the High One and shall crush the saints of the Most High. And he shall think himself able to change times and laws; and they shall be delivered into his hand until a time and times and half a time.*

"And the remedy for this is true spiritual fervor, praying day and night. As Saint Luke says: *You ought always to pray and not to faint.*

"*Et nunc dixi vobis priusquam fiat . . .*"

The sermon may last for two, three or more hours but no one notices the flight of time. In the first place the voice of the speaker is so arresting, perfect in its quality, perfect in modulation, perfect in its natural simplicity. In the second place, the matter of his sermon is always of vital interest, suited to his audience, lightened by anecdote, sparkling with humor. He is speaking to his 'good friends' and so between the preacher and his auditors there is forged a strong chain. In the third place he can be heard distinctly by all, even those on the outskirts of the crowd and, a second miracle, whatever their nationality they can all understand him.

And so they stand, hour after hour, whoever and wherever they may be, hanging on his words, rapt, carried out of themselves, weeping, calling on God for mercy, baring their shoulders to the discipline. When the preacher ends at last with a great Sign of the Cross, there is a moment's silence, and then the vast crowd breaks up into groups, moving here and there, seeking those priests who follow Father Vincent as Confessors.

The friar comes down from the platform and, moving towards the group of sick gathered close under the scaffolding, he blesses them, healing one after the other in their tens and hundreds.

Now there is another movement in the throng, the magistrates of the town are coming to claim their visitor. All manner of persons are seeking his advice; some are in spiritual difficulties and some need his help in temporal matters. He listens to the first comer with gentle, patient attention and then passes on to the next, advising, admonishing, correcting according to the needs of each.

The chief official comes bustling up. He has prepared a feast, every one has made a contribution, and Master Vincent must honor them by dining with them. With the same gracious patience, he follows his host, is taken to the municipal hall and seated in the place of honor. Here tact is necessary, for the friar has so long been accustomed to fasting that a feast is a physical impossibility. He must contrive to pour water into his cup so that a few drops of wine may fill it; his hosts must be kept so interested in the flow of conversation that they do not notice their guest toying with his food; for he must so manage that one, or at the most two, dishes shall last him throughout the meal.

Then a messenger comes into the hall, it is time to move on and Father Vincent's company, augmented by a couple of hundred or so of today's audience, is waiting for him. The master comes out and mounts his little she-ass; then towards the westering sun they march, chanting and praying, while those left behind regretfully watch the cloud of dust disappear into the red-gold of the horizon.

# Chapter II

## *The Unfolding of the Parable*

The life of an apostle has a twofold meaning. First, it is meant to be an accurate account of the events of his life—valuable as an historical and biographical document. But also, and even more important, the life of an apostle is a parable teaching a lesson to the men of his time and the men of all times. As an historical document should be as accurate as possible, but as a parable it is not in the least necessary that the life be factually accurate in every detail. Therefore, the wonders of our saint's life, even though they are for the greater part juridically attested, have their greatest importance as a lesson for other men. Nor does this lesson lose its validity if a few of the details have been supplied by legend instead of by history.

Thus, in its greater importance, Vincent Ferrer's life is a parable to be read in the light of our own times, a prophecy which concerns this, the middle of the twentieth century. There is the man, his message, and the signs which attested the truth of the message. These make one connected whole and are God's message to us here and now as truly as they

14

were in 1400. *Unless you do penance, you shall all likewise perish.*

Though one or the other detail may be inaccurate, certainly Vincent Ferrer's life was marked by preternatural gifts. These gifts, graces given for the benefit of others, are the seal of the King on the mission of His servants and, since they do not of themselves contribute to the personal sanctity of the wonder-worker, they may profitably be left to occupy their own place in the general scene. Strange, breath-taking as they are, almost incredible to our sophisticated minds, let them stand just as they are related. The message Vincent had to deliver was amazing enough in all conscience; it was terribly urgent, and so it had to be thrown into high light by these breath-taking miracles.

Vincent Ferrer was the fourth child, the second son, of a family of eight. His father was a lawyer of repute in Valencia and both he and his wife, Christina, were people of exemplary life. The elder brother, Pedro, grew up to become a respected business man of the city; Boniface, the younger, had a much more varied career. He was trained in his father's profession, married, and practiced the law for some years. On the death of his wife, following the advice of his elder brother Vincent, he became a Carthusian, being eventually elected General of that portion of the Order which followed the Avignonese obedience. He and his Dominican brother shared many of the political activities which the exigencies of the times forced on both of them.

The birth of this fourth child of a city lawyer was a matter of much interest and excitement in Valencia, for it was heralded by portents. One night, some weeks before his birth, the father dreamed that he was listening to a sermon,

15

the preacher being a Dominican well-known to him. Suddenly, the speaker interrupted himself to announce the approaching birth of one who would be a Dominican and the glory of Spain. At this the congregation all rose to pay homage to the unborn child.

Dona Christina was accustomed to give a monthly dole of flour to a poor blind woman. On coming with her alms, she asked the woman to pray for her safe delivery. Leaning her head against the breast of her benefactor, the poor woman was beginning to assure her of her prayers for her safety, when she suddenly broke off to cry aloud: "The child you bear has restored my sight," which indeed proved to be the case.

Pregnancy had always been difficult for Christina but this child brought only health and general well-being. When labor pains came on her the father went to the parish church to pray for his wife, and when they brought news of her safety and the birth of a son, he gave thanks to God.

By this time interest in the city had grown so keen that nothing would serve the people but that two of the chief magistrates and one of the best born of the ladies should stand sponsor to the child. So on the very evening of his birth, the baby was carried in state to the parish church of Saint Stephen, accompanied by the whole court of magistrates in their robes of ceremony.

When they reached the church, however, a dispute arose as to who should have the privilege of naming the child. As none of them had the slightest intention of giving way it looked as if the sojourn in the church might be indefinitely prolonged; but the parish priest, En Perot Pertusa, found a solution by declaring that he himself would name the child after the patron saint of Valencia, Saint Vincent, Martyr. This apparently satisfied all parties and

16

the baby was baptized Vincent without any more ado.

He was a very good baby, still, silent and very placid, more like an alabaster bambino than a child of flesh and blood. For his mother's peace of mind this was as well, for during the months of his infancy there was no falling off in the interest which the whole town showed in the Ferrer baby. Everyone came to the house in the Calle del Mar, on the road leading to the port, and so Dona Christina had visitors all day long. The climax, however, was reached when the Queen of Aragon sent orders that the Ferrer baby was to be brought to the palace for inspection.

While he was still an infant in arms, just beginning to babble, there fell a season of drought in Aragon, followed as usual by famine and pestilence. One day Dona Christina was nursing her child and praying as she did so for God's mercy on the country, when she distinctly heard the baby say:

"Carry me in the procession if you wish for rain."

Amazed and frightened, the mother, nevertheless, took the child with her in the next intercessory procession, and as he had foretold, rain fell in abundance.

There was a well in the garden, a stone curb surrounding a spring. One day, when he was three or four years old, little Vincent was playing on the brink of the well. It is difficult to imagine how he came to be left alone in such a place, but the fact remains that he was there and alone.

Following the custom of small children, he pulled off one of his shoes and began to play with the shoe and his bare toes. It was not long before he had contrived to throw the shoe into the well. Crawling to the edge and looking over, he could see his foot-gear below on the water far out of reach. An ordinary child would have set up a howl, but Vincent was imperturbable. There

17

was no screaming, no tears. Someone arrived on the scene at the moment, probably to look for the truant, and saw him make the Sign of the Cross over the well. Then the water gradually rose until it reached the edge of the curb, when the shoe floated to the side. Its small owner retrieved it perfectly dry and put it on again.

From this time on the well never dried up, and in the seasons of drought so common in Spain, people would come there from all over the town to draw water.

In common with the rest of God's saints, little Vincent had a great love of the poor. His mother, a truly charitable woman herself, inculcated this virtue early in her children. As we read in one of his sermons:

*From the sermons; on love of the poor. (Some of St. Vincent's sermons w e r e obviously notes taken by one present. This is an example.)*

"As the mother of Master Vincent taught her son, alms must be given with compassion, for Christ came to Jerusalem to bestow the alms of His teaching, and His works of mercy both spiritual and corporal by healing sinners and sick. It is a far greater mercy to give his sight to a blind man in alms than a florin. Now Christ was first moved by compassion, for seeing the city He wept over it; and so He taught the rich that they ought to give alms to the poor in spirit by compassionating their poverty and need, before they bestow temporal alms.

"This is the second reason why Christ wept over Jerusalem; for He knew how many were poor in the righteousness of their lives, poor in holiness, poor in devotion. He knew likewise how many were poor in health, poor in sight, hearing and speech. And so He compassionated before healing. A penny given in this way, with compassion, is worth far more than a florin given from the purse only and not from the heart."

Vincent's father likewise encouraged the child's generosity;

18

and if neither parent were available, or the matter was beyond their remedying, then a miracle would solve the dilemma; in fact, from very early years, the working of miracles was a normal event in his everyday life.

One of his playmates, the small son of a friend of his father's, contracted an infection which resulted in a very bad abscess on his neck. Vincent laid his hand on the sore, which immediately dried up; then, following a childish custom, common in all ages and countries, he kissed it to make it well, and there was left not so much as the smallest scar.

When he was eight years old he was sent, poor child, to study grammar, rhetoric and the humanities. By the time he had reached his fifteenth year he had mastered dialectic. In six years he had completed his course of studies. Piety set its vivifying seal on his whole being, the practice of mortification, by curbing his body, set the spirit free; and so, youthful exuberance, which passion either claims as its servant or obeys as its master, served to quicken the intelligence, since penance forbade it to release his sensitive passions.

Nevertheless, he was no mere bookish student, purblind and narrow in outlook. Purity of soul quickened his sense of beauty and he loved the glories of God's world; he loved the country-side, above all he loved the sea. By the shore, on his knees as if he were in a temple, his soul opened wide to the God who spoke by His works. In the limpid blue of the sea, in the perfumed peace of a summer evening, he listened to the thousand sounds which arose from the fruitful earth, its hymn of life, breathing its love of its Creator. Then he would join his heart to the stars circling in an immense orb of prayer.

If he were out with companions, turning to them he would say:

"What a good Father we have in heaven! To save us from the temptation of seeking the poor miserable pleasures of the world, He has filled the sky with beauties to remind us of the wonderful loveliness of our real Home. If the sun is so magnificently awe-inspiring, if the moon is so softly radiant, how marvellous it will be when we see the light of Our Lord, the Sun of Justice. How beautiful will be Our Lady, Mary, the heavenly Moon in its zenith, the pure Dawn of Grace. Imagine the saints shining like stars in the sky! There, in all its fulness, we shall find unfading joy."

Of course there were times when he got on people's nerves. The saints stand out in such exceedingly sharp contrast to the generality of mankind, that folk in the clutches of bad humor, or yielding to the seductions of their animal nature find in their very presence a tacit rebuke.

One day Vincent came on the scene to hear one of his father's servants venting his spleen in language which stung the very air round him. This was more than the lad could stand and so he told the man to be quiet. It was a match to tinder, and the exasperated servant swinging round struck his young master a blow in the face. Sobered at once before such an unheard-of act of insolence, the frightened man was beginning an apology, but Vincent stopped him.

"Don't trouble about it," he said. "I did wrong in speaking so to one so much older than myself. And in any case to correct someone who has lost self-mastery only makes matters worse. As for the blow, forget all about it, as I shall. No one else need ever know."

Some of Vincent's contemporaries, young men about town, found it very difficult to regard him seriously. Such a very old head on such very young shoulders seemed to

20

them no more than a matter for mirth. Besides, there were these miracles that people were always talking about; they had never seen him work a miracle, and they did not altogether believe in them. It would be good fun to play a practical joke. Young Ferrer was such a simpleton, his wits always woolgathering, no one knew where, that it would be easy to hoodwink him. Let one of them pretend to fall down dead somewhere in his vicinity; then the rest could fetch young Ferrer up to the supposed corpse and ask him to work a miracle. He was an obliging simpleton and would certainly begin his prayers at once. Then the pretended corpse would come to life, there would be a tremendous flutter among the bystanders, and when the amazement and excitement had gone far enough they would tell the real facts and there would be a fine laugh against this paragon about whom their elders made such a ridiculous fuss.

So they watched him go out of the city gate one evening and then lay in wait. As soon as they saw him returning, one of them lay down by the roadside as they had planned, while the others rushed out to the gate shouting and crying:

"Vincent Ferrer! Vincent Ferrer! Come quick. A man has just fallen dead by the side of the road. Come and bring him back to life." And as the youths were no mean actors, their grief and consternation were very realistic indeed.

Vincent looked at the young men, looked at them with a grave direct scrutiny which they somehow found disconcerting. They began to wonder uneasily whether this moonstruck devotee was such a simpleton after all. However, they had begun the farce and there was nothing for it but to carry it through to the end.

21

Still crying and gesticulating, though the heart had gone from the game, they brought him to the place where the pretended corpse lay on its face. Vincent stood beside it for a moment, still silent and still with that look of disconcerting gravity on his face. At last he broke the silence, and his words were even more disconcerting than his silence had been.

"This is reality and no practical joke."

The tension was becoming unbearable; the lads could stand it no longer; one stirred his prostrate companion with his foot:

"Get up," he said gruffly, "the joke is not working."

But the prostrate body did not move and, seriously alarmed, two or three knelt down to pull their companion to his feet. But there was no response, so they lifted the body and laid it on its back. Still no movement. Terrified hands felt for the still heart. Death was there in stark reality. As Vincent had said, this was no practical joke.

Sick with fear, horror and shame, the lads fell on their knees at Vincent's feet begging his pardon, and entreating him, imploring him, to show his power and to give back his life to the companion whose sin after all was no greater than theirs.

Making the Sign of the Cross over the lifeless body, Vincent passed on without another word into the city, while the dead youth sat up, rubbed his eyes, and looked in bewilderment round him.

# Chapter III

## *The Training of an Apostle*

From the day of his birth his parents had made up their minds that their son Vincent should be a priest. There was no question, of course, of forcing a vocation; the lad was to make his own choice, but, from his earliest years, the choice was influenced by his parents' manifest desires. At the age of seven he was given the tonsure, a provisional step; and at the age of eleven he received a small benefice, the Chapel of Saint Ann. As soon as he had ended his studies, a family conclave began to consider the details of his future.

Parental plans probably envisaged a canon's stall, the life of a worthy, learned, dignified ecclesiastic. Studying the ecclesiastical history of the time and the lives of many, even of high dignity in the Church, to have a good canon or priest for a son was no mean ambition. But to it Vincent's own determination was diametrically opposed. He told his parents:

"I have no interest whatever in money or in any sort of position. I only ask for your blessing and permission to go to the Friars Preachers."

23

The father made no demur, but Christina, though outwardly acquiescent, was far from satisfied. This son of hers, so brilliant—what a name he could make for himself; and now to bury his talents among mendicant friars!

Yet she let him go, and one day Vincent went to the priory in the town to beg admission; he went, as he had hoped, as an ordinary postulant. But his coming was not to be so unobtrusive as he intended; never through life was he to be allowed to sink himself, to hide himself. Saint Dominic had been there beforehand, and in a vision had warned the prior that he was going to receive a new subject who would one day be the glory of Spain. The community knew this, and accordingly when he arrived on February 2, 1367, young Vincent was exciting an interest of which he was totally unaware. Neither did anyone enlighten him; for the sake of his community no one is allowed to think himself different or in any way better than the rest.

He began his novitiate, and for some years little more is known of the young man. The priory records speak of his unfeigned humility, his tireless prayer, his unwearied assiduity in every duty, and his serene affability of manner. "He was never to be seen standing about in idleness, or wasting his time in useless talk. He was full of a great and wonderful humility, and was in all things the perfection of manhood (*se omnibus Humanus exibebat*)." With the greatest diligence he studied the life of his Father in God, Saint Dominic, so that at last he became indeed a true son, the pattern and model of his Father.

He had the greatest love for his cell; and this love, gained in the peace of the novitiate, stood him in good stead later, when his life became one ceaseless round of toil, exteriorized until only a saint could have preserved in silence of soul the one thing that mattered. To the day of

24

his death he was able in all truth to say: "Where my cell is there is my heaven." It was there that on his return he would find that the word in the manuscript, which at the call of obedience he had left unfinished, had been completed in letters of gold. It was there that the thread of inspiration, broken at the same call, would return to him as the dove came back to Noah in the ark. There, in the glance so often exchanged with his crucifix, he found that intimacy of love which is the whole motive power of the religious life. That every man makes his own image is a true saying. Vincent was content to be merely the marble, leaving it to God Almighty to be the Sculptor. No wonder that all recognized in him a follower of Christ.

But the year of simple novitiate was not to pass without a trial. We have seen that Christina Ferrer had never really acquiesced in her son's becoming a friar. Time did not soften her heartache, and throughout the year a burning desire to regain her brilliant son grew until her longing became more than she could bear. So one day she went to the priory and asked to see Vincent.

She opened her attack with a woman's strongest weapon, tears. Having thus unmasked her batteries, she proceeded to bring all her persuasive powers to bear. God knew, as she did, that this son of hers, buried in the priory, was wasting talents which were, after all, God-given. It was his plain duty, she had scripture warrant, Our Lord's own words for it, that he ought so to let his light shine before men that they might honor their Father who is in heaven. Of course he was to be a priest, no one could wish for this more than she did, but he must be a secular priest making the name of Ferrer illustrious through the length and breadth of Spain. So she talked, and talked, and Vincent listened in silence.

25

The young novice loved his mother, he revered her goodness. Perhaps, after all, she was in the right, God's mouthpiece, telling him what was really the divine will in his regard. As he listened and pondered, he seemed to himself to be floating away on a sea of peace; he was at rest, enveloped in a dreamy, delicious languor. Surely this sense of peace was a divine token. Christina watching him with a mother's clear-sighted eyes, saw his expression change, and was content. Being a wise woman she felt she had said enough for one day, and so rising, she bade him farewell and left.

Still more than half hypnotized, Vincent went back to his beloved cell. There was bracing austerity in the bare little cubicle in the common dormitory. On a small table lay his work, above it hung his crucifix. All around him, in similar cells brother novices were reading, writing, studying, praying. Now he saw aright. He knew he had been facing subtle temptation, and he knew also that, for the moment, he had been in danger of yielding. He fell on his knees.

"You, my God, You and Your blessed will," he cried, his tears falling fast. "You alone my portion for ever." He rose, once more his own master, his will strengthened to his purpose.

Next morning, still more than satisfied with the turn events had taken on the previous day, Dona Christina returned to her charge at the priory and asked for her son. Vincent came at once, loving, kind, cheerful, just as he always was. But the mother knew at once that she had lost her battle. Vincent's will, entrenched behind granite determination to follow his vocation, was impregnable. To combat any more was useless. By pressing him too far she risked losing all in losing his friendship. She soon rose and came away, beating back all her trouble until she could hide herself to cry unnoticed in a quiet corner of the church.

When she came out into the porch again, all tear-be-draggled, a beggar man spoke to her.

"Why are you crying?" he asked; and Dona Christina, still too immersed in her own griefs to notice or be offended at the strangeness of the address, began to tell him all that had befallen her. She spoke of her son almost as one speaks of the dead, of her pride in him and her hopes for him and how all had been disappointment; she told how nearly she had gained her own way and how this made the thwarting of her desires still more bitter.

Then, by degrees she began, without meaning to do so, to change her theme. She saw him as the child he used to be, her good son. She recalled the prodigies of his birth and the miracles which had dropped like flowers from his fingers.

And as she talked it was borne in on her quite clearly that she had not lost her son, but had, on the contrary, gained something much greater. She raised her eyes to express her new sentiment, and as she did so she realized with something of a shock that she had been talking thus intimately with a stranger and a beggar. A generous alms was the only return—a miserably inadequate one—that she could make.

Opening her purse, she turned to give him all its contents with the most gracious thanks she could offer. But the beggar had disappeared, he was no longer beside her; nor, though she searched the length of the sunny street could she find him.

On the sixth of February in the year 1368, Vincent Ferrer made his profession. With his hands between those of his prior, he promised obedience to the representative of the master general until death.

27

# CHAPTER IV

## Student and Teacher

Brother Vincent was professed, as we have said, on February 6, 1368, and from that time until the General Chapter held at Tarragona in September of the same year, his prior entrusted him with the giving of a series of lectures on philosophy to which extern students were admitted. He must have begun to make his mark among his brethren early, since he was not yet ordained.

The General Chapter assigned him to the Studium Generale at Barcelona to take a course in logic, not because he was ignorant of the science in question, but that he might study Dominican methods of exposition. From Barcelona he was sent in 1370 to the provincial House of Studies at Lerida, to teach under supervision (as lector in logic) what he had already learnt.

When his term as lector was ended, the provincial again sent him to Barcelona, this time to study the sacred Scriptures, not only the Bible and the commentaries of the doctors, but also the Hebrew language. In 1374, he was still living in the Convent of Saint Catherine at Barcelona, and it was there that his apostolic work saw its beginning; 1374 witnessed also the commencement of an era of prodigies which only ended with his death.

During this year, as the result of drought and several bad harvests, the Kingdom of Aragon suffered severely from famine and the pestilence which always followed in its wake. Vessels laden with corn were sent from Sardinia, but the Signoria of the island of Majorca, also in the throes of famine, gave orders that all grain ships should be intercepted and brought into port there. The Valencian sailors complained to the king of these acts of piracy, and the king gave orders for ships for the relief of the stricken province to be dispatched from Flanders. But it seemed as though the elements themselves were in league against the unfortunate Aragonese, for it was March, the season of storms, and though the starving people waited and watched, no ships came in sight.

Then Vincent, who was already beginning to be known in Barcelona as a preacher, spoke to the townsfolk, advising them to beg for the divine mercy by organizing intercessory processions. They took his advice—after all it was their great resource in time of trouble—and the following Sunday, processions from all parts of the town converged on the great square where Vincent preached to them, his audience numbering twenty thousand.

He told them first that this famine was in punishment of their sins and exhorted them to repentance; then he urged them to great confidence in the mercy of God who only struck in order to heal. Suddenly, as he was speaking, his face lighted up.

"Have confidence," he cried, "rejoice in God. Before night two ships laden with corn will make port, the harbingers of abundant supplies."

29

This prophecy was very ill-received, for the weather gave no sign of improvement, and in the circumstances it was impossible for any vessel to make port. The people were very angry: the preacher, they said, was no better than an empty babbler, and to make mockery in this way of the sufferings of others was in the worst possible taste. His brethren at the priory were even more annoyed, and told him in no measured terms. The prior said to him:

"For the future, Brother Vincent, you may dispense yourself from making any sort of prophecy, anything in fact which singles you out from the rest of the community. Singularity is a curse which leads to spiritual pride and the death of the soul."

Vincent bowed his head in acquiescence. To speak was forbidden him, he could only pray that God in His mercy would overlook the incredulity of those to whom he was bringing help.

When the evening began to draw in, against all probability two sails appeared on the horizon, and, still greater marvel, they were making for Barcelona. The sentinel on guard at the castle of Mont-Juich signalled their approach, and when they reached harbor it was found that they were indeed ships from Flanders laden with grain.

The people of Barcelona, after the first transports of joy were over, divided between admiration and terror, did not know what to think. Their imaginations were fired by the thought of the young prophet, but only too conscious of their many crimes they feared his power and the mystery which surrounded him. How much did he know with his preternatural powers? Had he not also the power to call down on them the vengeance of God? They followed him, they went to all his sermons, but in great awe. Brother Vincent, too, was not at his ease, he felt diffident and anxious. God had given him great powers but he had been forbidden to use them, for even after the fulfillment of his prophecy the prior had not revoked his prohibition. Could he be always sure that he would not inadvertently be guilty of disobedience? And was not obedience better than sacrifice? His fear was not without foundation.

One day he happened to be passing through a street where a prison was in process of building. As he came in sight a mason on the scaffolding missed his footing, overbalanced and fell.

"Brother Vincent, save me," cried the unfortunate man.

Vincent remembered; obedience was greater even than alms deeds, and charity he knew took its value from obedience; he could not help the man unless the prior gave him leave to do so.

"Stay where you are," he shouted, "until I come back." Immediately the mason stopped falling and remained hanging in mid air, while a gaping crowd gathered beneath.

Hurrying back to the priory, Vincent sought his superior:

"A mason who is falling off a roof has asked me to help him. He is waiting until I have your permission."

"Waiting?" gasped the prior.

"Yes," said Vincent calmly. Whatever was the prior looking so astonished about? He must know that Vincent could not save him without permission, and in common humanity he could not let the man be dashed to pieces because he could not run fast enough. The prior took a deep breath. He must have felt a little like a very small hedge-sparrow when it first finds a young cuckoo hatched from the egg lying among its own. Vincent was incorrigible in his simplicity. Shrugging his shoulders, divided between admiration, irritation and amusement, the prior answered.

"Go back and finish it off," he said resignedly, "since the miracle is already worked, and the street full of people."

Somewhat downcast and distressed, Vincent went back to the mason, who had remained all the time obediently suspended in mid-air.

"The prior says you may come down," he told him. And the man at once floated gently earthward.

In 1377 we find our friar again a student, this time at the famous school of studies in Toulouse, where he obtained his doctor's degree. A year later, he left Toulouse for his native city of Valencia and there, his studies ended, he began the work of preaching in earnest. His success there was immense. Teyxidor says of his preaching: "Vincent Ferrer carried out his mission with immeasurable success; to the great benefit of his audience, he mingled with the authority of his preaching the still greater authority of his example. On the days when he was going to preach, all the people in the surrounding country-side flocked to hear him, and not one of his auditors left him without feeling in his own heart some sparks of the fire which burned in the heart of the apostle; the credit, the renown, the veneration which he inspired reached such a pitch, that in Valencia, a gathering-place of distinguished people, there was in the opinion of the inhabitants only one religious, only one intellectual, only one saint, only one servant of Jesus Christ, and that one was Vincent Ferrer."

But prophecy and miraculous powers are only the outward and accidental trappings of sanctity. The vital, the necessary matter is the union of the soul in charity with God: abounding joy in His presence, alternating with anxious search for a hidden Lover; crucified love of a crucified Spouse; the begetting of souls in God as the fruit of such union. The veil which hides Vincent Ferrer's inner life is, for the most part, closely drawn. Only now and then are we enabled to gain a glimpse of what passes in its hidden depths.

After Matins, Brother Vincent was accustomed to pray instead of going to his cell. To conquer sleep and excite devotion he had a custom very similar to that which Blessed Henry Suso had practiced and for the same purpose. He used to make a kind of Stations of the Cross, visiting the altars in the Church, or the statues in the long, cold cloisters.

One night after he had spent a long time in meditation on the sufferings of Our Lord, he went to a large crucifix and, kneeling there, carried clean out of himself by the thought of Our Lord's love for him, he stretched out both arms to the crucifix saying:

"Is it possible, my Lord, that you have suffered so much for me?" Immediately the arms detached themselves, and the figure on the Cross leaned forward with Vincent's own gesture:

"Yes, and more than this," answered the Crucified.

The devil, ever busy to fill hell, infuriated by innocence and repentance, was not going to leave the friar at peace in his work for souls. One night, as Vincent was praying, he was accosted by an old man of venerable appearance clothed in sackcloth. He was gaunt and emaciated, with a long white beard falling to his waist, in fact, a typical Father of the Desert. This old man told Vincent that he was a hermit who had come to see and speak with him.

The upshot of a long discourse was that it was wicked in a young man like the friar to ruin health and strength as he was doing by fasts and vigils. After all, prudence was one of the cardinal virtues, and by the exercise of prudence the old hermit had contrived to reach the heights of contemplative sanctity while, throughout a long life, he

33

had likewise managed to enjoy all its pleasures, for the two were not incompatible. At first the young man, taken by surprise, was inclined to accept his visitor's suggestions, but the discourse had not lasted long before the trained mind perceived its many discrepancies. Vincent knew to whom he was speaking, and an imperious gesture put the fiend to flight.

On another occasion, the devil appeared in the guise of a savage threatening him with war to the death. After that, for a while, temptations to despair, temptations of the flesh, temptations to lassitude and heart-weariness, all bore him down so heavily that at last, in sheer terror, he called on Mary, his mother, begging her to save him lest he perish. Then, through the lips of one of her statues, she deigned to strengthen and console him.

Unable to conquer Vincent by assaults of this kind, the devil set in his path snares of another nature. Women change but little throughout the ages; there always has been, and there always will be, a proportion of their number who make the practice of piety and religion a kind of game. Religious life is their hobby, and so they join every sort of guild or confraternity they can find, seeking excitement in fancying themselves in the inner circle, so to speak. They talk in half sentences of Father This and Father That, hinting at deep and special knowledge of mysteries which are not for the generality. May heaven preserve us from the woman who talks of "My Director!" It means nothing, but does an infinitude of mischief among the ignorant and simple. Later on in life, Friar Vincent managed his women penitents with consummate skill, as we shall see.

At this time, however, he was too utterly simple and candid to realize how foolish some women may be. A young girl of noble birth, Inez Fernandez, moved by desire of

excitement and love of novelty, became one of his penitents. Sentimentality, indulged in and allowed to run riot,
led to worse, and the silly girl fell in love with her confessor. Vincent, entirely unconscious of the turn affairs
had taken, found his penitent a great nuisance, but being a
saint he put up with her. At length, Inez, casting self-control to the winds, on finding that she was not making the
slightest impression on her confessor, decided to pretend
that she was seriously ill in order that she might have a
pretext for sending for him.

Vincent answered the call, for the salvation of souls was
his business, and he had no notion that there was more
behind. He came into the girl's room prepared to hear her
confession, only to discover that it was not sacramental confession, but one of an entirely different kind, for which she
had sent for him. She had reached a state of mind where
she had become utterly shameless. Vincent heard the beginning, and then, turning on his heel, without another word,
left the room.

Inez was furious; her hot southern temper changed love
in a twinkling to hatred, and she set about planning revenge. But before she had time to accomplish anything her
sin brought its own punishment; she had abandoned self-
control and so the devil took what she had abandoned.
She became a dangerous maniac. Exorcisms were tried in
vain.

"Do what you will," said the devil by the mouth of
the wretched girl, "I will not go out except at the command of him who passed through fire without being
scorched."

So the girl's friends went to Vincent as the only one
who might be able to read the riddle. The friar knew and
at first he hesitated, for he did not like notoriety; but char-

ity called and so he went at once to the Fernandez house.

"Here he comes," shrieked the fiend, "the man whom fire could not burn." Entering the room, Vincent commanded the devil to leave the possessed woman. Shrieking horribly and tearing his victim, the evil spirit departed, leaving the girl sane in mind but half dead in body.

Another time, a person to whom the friar's life was a constant rebuke, introduced a professional harlot into his cell. This time Vincent did not run away; he remained to convert the poor creature.

About this time, another friar was in a difficulty. He had been guilty of misconduct and feared a public scandal. Thinking only of himself and not at all of the disgrace he was bringing on his convent, he persuaded his accomplice to go to the city magistrates to denounce Friar Vincent.

It happened that Vincent's brother, Boniface, was of their number. He was perfectly convinced that the whole tale was a lie but he wished to prove it to the satisfaction of the rest so that, once and for all, gossip might be stopped. So he persuaded his brother magistrates to call a public procession for the following Sunday, knowing that all the religious of the city would take part.

When the time came, Boniface and some of his fellow magistrates took the woman to a place where she could see everything. The procession filed past and presently Vincent came in sight. The woman made no sign. Boniface turned to her.

"There goes the man of whom you have made complaint," he remarked.

"That is not he," answered the woman promptly, "I know that friar well by sight and he is a saint."

Just at this time life was difficult in many ways for Vincent. It seemed to him that he was the butt of all evil tongues both in and outside the priory. It was the tempering of the sword. Shortly God was to use him many wonderful ways. Gold must be purified in the furnace; and before they are apt for His purpose, God's elect must also be purified in a fire which is even more searching because it is unseen.

# Chapter V

## His First Teaching

If Vincent Ferrer is not counted among the great masters of the spiritual life it is because his immense apostolate, and his authority among popes, princes, and kings has overshadowed everything else. His sermons are his gift to posterity, but there is also a treatise which should find a place with the *Imitation* and *The Spiritual Combat.* This work, *The Treaty of the Spiritual Life,* has evidently been written for the instruction of his brethren. When it was written no one can tell. Perhaps in his early days, perhaps when he was prior, perhaps at Avignon, perhaps again in his old age. But the time of its first appearance is immaterial; its right place in this book is here and for a reason which he himself gives as the first proposition. "You can only give what you yourself possess. In fact, you must have much more than you attempt to give, to enable you to give without despoiling yourself."

*From* The Treaty of the Spiritual Life. The first chapter treats of poverty: *"Blessed are the poor. Then be truly poor. There are no earthly goods which are*

38

worth a thought; in fact, it would be truer to say that there are no goods in this world, only needs, that is to say, miseries. Then curb your needs as far as you can, and only take what is absolutely necessary. If at times you suffer from hunger and thirst, what is that but the habitual lot of the poor. When those to whom you preach see that you are truly poor in spirit, they will be more surely moved to generosity than by the most eloquent sermon if the preacher does not practice what he commends."

Concerning silence: "Peace and happiness are so closely connected as to be almost one and the same thing. Our Master said: *My peace I leave you. My peace I give to you.* It was a peace that He paid dearly to acquire for us. After attachment to the goods of this world, there is nothing so destructive to peace as an unbridled tongue; therefore, keep silence. Speak only by way of answer and then only concerning serious matters. To go deeper still, do not even think useless thoughts. Nothing except sin should ever trouble you. Misfortunes? Such do not even exist for you. Human wickedness? If it were not for the grace of God you would be worse than any. What right have you to judge? Your life ought to be a continual exercise in suffering for your divine Master, who leads the way for you in love of suffering. That is why, as soon as you perceive in yourself the least desire to dominate others, you must crush it as pitilessly in its beginnings as you would crush a viper under foot.

"You must open the interior eyes of your soul on this light, on this heaven within you, a vast horizon stretching far beyond the realm of human activity, an unexplored country to the majority of men. The ordinary observer sees in the ocean only the realm of storms, and never guesses that a few feet below the surface its waters are always

39

limpid, and in a scintillating clarity is found vegetation and living creatures of wondrous diversity, marvellous in beauty and structure, mysterious depths where the pearl is formed.

"Such is the depth of the soul where God dwells and shows Himself to us. And when the soul has seen God, what more can it want? If it possesses Him, why and for whom can it ever be moved to abandon Him?

"So, at any price, preserve yourself in that calm through which the soul sees the eternal Sun. This vision of God will also show you yourself. The heights of greatness will show you the depths of misery. But fear nothing, consider this misery at your leisure; it is your work in the world to place this rebellious nonentity which is yourself in contrast to the source of all being, God. When you have realized your true worth you will be able to judge your faults sanely, your own crimes will come home to you in full light, and the faults of your neighbor will remain in shadow.

"When the soul, after having thus put at a distance all earthly things, reverts to herself and so enters on a happy recovery, she begins to draw near to original justice, and the eye of interior contemplation dilates. She sees in herself a mysterious ladder by which she mounts to the sight of spiritual being, first the angels and then God. In this vision her heart is inflamed and the things of earth are lost in a happy distance; charity embraces her, and at last its ardent fire destroys in the soul anything which remains either of stain or of vanity.

"Having reached this point of the interior life a man may now go and preach to others. Material goods are nothing to him. As for vainglory, he knows what he is before God, and he knows even better, that without the divine assistance he cannot so much as pronounce the ineffable name."

In the chapter on purification of heart and mortification of the senses and passions, by which a man obtains purity of soul, Vincent lays much stress on fidelity to the rule and constitutions.  He says:

"Do no more and no less than is ordained for you, in the choir, the refectory, the dormitory; in the inclinations, prostrations, manner of standing and sitting.  Everything has been foreseen and arranged for you, see that you follow it out.  This is how you will make your body, by nature a terrible obstacle to your salvation, a living holocaust to the Lord.  This is how you fulfil your vow to be obedient to death, to the death of yourself in everything.  It is through this obedience to the death of yourself that you will, in your grateful humility, count your daily victories.  Freed from the care of your body, whose least movement is thus withdrawn from the idle breath of caprice, your soul will rise on wings of love and prayer."

*(Through page 46) From* **The Treaty** *of the* **Spiritual** *Life.*

From the heights of loving detachment, Vincent does not consider it superfluous to descend to practical details.

At table for instance: "The soul should be master, for this is a point on which body and soul are in close alliance.  Do not forsake the safe mean either by excess or defect.  Study your own temperament.  Discover whether you lean towards self-indulgence or ill-regulated austerity.  A safe rule to follow is to eat sufficient to be able to study or pray afterwards, neither faint from unsatisfied hunger, nor be torpid from overeating.

"Do not deprive yourself of bread, and eat a sufficiency of whatever else is offered you.  The fasts of the Order and the manner of observing them should be your rule.  In the refectory eat only of what is served to everybody; be inexorable in refusing anything provided for yourself alone.  But if you are unwell, then accept whatever is necessary for you, receiving with gratitude whatever extra may be given you, but never procure anything for yourself.

"With regard to drinking, this matter is more difficult to regulate. Aim at drinking as little as possible, but this little must be sufficient to prevent your suffering from thirst either by day or by night. Do not drink between meals except in case of extreme need. Always put water in your wine; with regard to the extent to which you should water it, God will inspire you.

"Before going to table bless God with all the powers of body and soul. Then seat yourself in fear, considering within yourself that you are going to eat the sins of the people. Before beginning to eat, say a *Pater* and *Ave* for the souls in purgatory who are farthest from God, and, for that reason, hunger most. From what is served choose the pieces which appeal the least to sensuality."

With regard to sleep (here you must remember that an insufficiency is as dangerous as excess): "Fear the snares of the evil one. To the man who is in need of sleep he will say: 'When will you expiate your sins unless you keep vigil?' To the man whose soul will benefit by keeping vigil, he will say: 'Do you not remember how tired you are? You will be good for nothing if you insist on watching as you do.' To obtain light in this matter consult God in fervent prayer; or, better still, sleep as long as the rule permits, and this advice includes the summer siesta. Do not prolong your vigils, to the end that you may rise the more easily for Matins and recite that Hour more joyously.

"Before sleeping, ruminate on some verses of a psalm, or dwell on some other pious thought; for example, on what passes during this hour of Our Lord's sacred Passion. For the rest, no one, however strong in spirit he may be, ought to omit anything which rouses devotion. When he reads or studies, his thought ought to turn frequently towards Christ, speaking to Him and asking understanding of Him.

"When the clock strikes, it is good to stop reading and close your eyes, to withdraw into the wounds of your Saviour. Sometimes it is good to rise, prostrate, and offer ardent prayers to God; or even to leave your cell, go to the church or chapter room according as the ardor of your spirit leads you. There, with the sighs and tears of a full heart, implore the divine assistance, presenting to the Most High your vows and desires, demanding with insistence that the saints help you by their prayers. And all this occurs without the help of set prayers although, usually, a man may help himself by using some passage of the sacred Scriptures or of some pious author. It is God who acts within. When this interior warmth has passed—and it commonly lasts but a short while—recall to your memory what you were studying previously, and you will find that you have gained marvellous enlightenment on the matter. Although there is no particular time when you may expect these interior movements, the phenomenon most often occurs in the morning. So do not stay up too late at night that your spirit may be better disposed to receive the divine touches in the morning.

"At the signal for Matins rise at once. Resting fully dressed on a hard bed should make this easy for you. Sing the psalms standing upright, your heart raised to God; put all your ardor into your prayers. Take care, nevertheless, that interior joy does not lead you to do anything out of order. Think of the angels who see Him face to face whom you only see in a dark manner. Do not neglect any detail of the Office however minute it may be. God will be the better pleased if you prepare it beforehand, so that you may

43

make no mistakes yourself, and may be able to supply for the mistakes of others, if such be needful. Nevertheless, modesty directs that you leave such correction to the elder Religious. Above all, do not enter into discussions on the matter; keep unalterable charity and humility. Spiritual unction will teach you the rest.

"Before all things, keep your eyes fixed on God and consider His attributes, then you will understand that what used to appear to you as honorable is as nothing compared with the infinite grandeur of His Majesty. Weigh well what Christ has suffered in body, mind and soul for love of you, and you will see that up to the present you have done nothing for Him.

"Think of the innocence and purity of life you have promised, of your strict duty to love God with all the powers of your soul, and how far you are from your goal. What have you done to show your gratitude for the benefits with which you have been overwhelmed? Raise your eyes to heaven and see the glory which is awaiting you there; what are your poor merits in comparison with that? What if you compare your life with those of the saints? and above all, if you consider the number and gravity of your offenses?

"God is preparing a rigorous and detailed judgment for each soul. Where are your works of virtue and penance? Perhaps tomorrow you will die; then how greatly will you long to have done more for the service of God. Whatever may be the degree in the spiritual life that you have reached, it is no more than a beginning which ought to be followed by constant efforts, active desires, for without such efforts and desires you will produce nothing but pride and presumption, such as will quickly lead you to a serious downfall. Watch yourself carefully, for there are great abysses into which men have fallen after they have reached a high

44

degree of sanctity, and all because of some unguarded inclination. Last of all, go down to hell in spirit and consider the punishment of the damned, and after that every penance, every punishment, will seem sweet to you."

But all these considerations are not merely a matter for the speculative intellect, they are, above all, an operation of the heart, which through love is the determining factor of the will.

This leads us to the seven forms of serving God, the seven forms of self-contempt, the seven forms of love of our neighbor.

"The seven forms of worshipping and serving God are: an ardent love, a sovereign fear, constant adoration, intense zeal, praise and thanksgiving, prompt and absolute obedience and, as far as possible, a taste for divine sweetness.

"The seven forms of self-contempt are: interior confusion at our faults, bitter and poignant sorrow for our sins, insomuch as they have offended God and stained our souls, practical and constant humility, the desire to be trodden under foot and to be looked on as the vilest of creatures, an unquenchable thirst for penance, an implacable hatred of the roots of our vices and perverse inclinations, a rigorous vigilance in keeping our senses and all the powers of our soul in the path of virtue, and lastly, perfect discretion, so that we do not exceed in anything.

"The seven forms of love of our neighbor are: a tender compassion which makes us feel his troubles as though they were our own, an affectionate participation in all the good which can befall him, tranquil endurance and forgiveness beforehand of any injury or annoyance he may cause us, constant friendliness in respect to everybody, humble reverence which leads us to look on everyone as our masters far better than we are, a cordial conformity with their sentiments and viewpoints so that we may truly make with them but one heart and soul in good, and finally an abiding disposition to offer ourselves for all, as Christ did and to work both day and night, that Christ may be King and Master in ourselves and in others."

# CHAPTER VI

## *The Great Schism of the West*

Writing the life of Saint Vincent Ferrer is a task beset with many difficulties which arise alike from his personal character and his unique mission. His life is so many-sided; it is like a diamond; each facet is so full of light and color that, finding every moment some new aspect of beauty, one turns the jewel round and round until one is almost stupified by the richness and variety which one meets at every angle. An author, unless intending to write a monumental work like that of Père Fages, is constrained to focus on one aspect, letting the rest group round this. Otherwise the thread which joins the whole is lost.

The whole book, for instance, might be written round the Great Schism of the West and our friar's connection with it. In point of fact, this aspect is so extremely important that, though I have gathered my threads in another pattern, I am constrained to give in briefest outline the part played by Vincent in this drama. I propose, therefore, to deal with this matter as briefly as possible in one chapter; and this will free me to leave it on one side, while I write from the particular angle I have chosen. If any reader wishes to go more deeply into the matter there are many other books available.

The schism which for forty years rent the seamless robe of the Church, Christ's Bride on earth, takes its rise in the "Babylonish Captivity" when, in 1309, the popes made Avignon their place of residence, and Rome was widowed of her bishop. In 1378, Saint Catherine of Siena persuaded Gregory XI to return to his bishopric; but his return, which might have meant so much to the Church, was followed almost immediately by the death of the pope.

The Romans were terrified at the thought of losing again what they had only just regained, and so when the cardinals assembled in Rome to elect a new pope, the populace gathered outside Saint Peter's threatening death to those inside if they did not elect a Roman. The cardinals temporized, saving their dignity and right of choice, while at the same time they tried to appease the people, by electing an Italian, Bartholomew Prignano, Archbishop of Bari, who took the name of Urban VI. Usually the cardinals proceeded immediately to enthrone the new pontiff, but on this occasion, knowing that they had only acceded in part to the wishes of the people, they hesitated to go farther than the bare act of election. The fears of some of them were even great enough to constrain them to leave the conclave and withdraw to the castle of Sant Angelo, behind walls capable of withstanding a siege.

The coronation, however, took place on Easter Sunday.

Urban was a good man, upright and austere, but he lacked tact and the charity that is kind. Everywhere reforms were urgently needed, but, as Saint Catherine of Siena pointed out to him, he must first win the hearts of his children before he could fruitfully reform them. Constitutionally impatient, Urban could not bring his mind to a slow advance. The cardinals saw what was coming; many of them were nervous of reform which could not fail to affect their own lives. So they repudiated the election on the grounds that since they had been constrained by fear of the Roman populace, they had not been free to vote as they choose and so there had been no valid election.

Urban, genuinely anxious to do the right thing, and to be as conciliatory as it was in his nature to be, left Rome for Anagni, intending to call the cardinals to a fresh consistory, hoping that this would at one and the same time confirm his election and dissipate all scruples. But these just hopes of peace were frustrated by the act of one unscrupulous woman greedy of power. Joanna, Queen of Naples, invited the dissident cardinals into her kingdom where, assembling in conclave at Fondi, they elected a new pope, Robert of Geneva, who took the name of Clement VII. The Great Schism had begun.

Although the Church has never formally pronounced on the matter, the general consensus of opinion among those who have studied the question exhaustively is that Urban was the true pope. Such is the general belief six hundred years after the event. But it is of common knowledge that to obtain a true perspective of anything it is necessary to stand at some distance from it. In too close a view the trees are apt to obscure the wood, and so it happened that contemporary judgment was divided fairly evenly between Urban and Clement. This was the case generally throughout the Church, for nations, princes, bishops, religious orders, all in good faith, declared some for Urban, some for Clement. There were two Dominican masters general, two ministers general of the Franciscans; Christendom was torn in two.

It may be a matter of surprise to some that there were canonized saints under either obedience; but it must be remembered that those who followed the antipope in good faith—and even now no one dares to affirm with absolute certainty which was the true pope—were guilty of no worse than an error of judgment, and errors of judgment in themselves are not sins meriting punishment. Divine Providence which, for its own good purposes, permitted the schism, did not leave the simple flock shepherdless, and that is one good reason why canonized saints are found under the obedience of Avignon as well as under that of Rome.

His sanctity, acknowledged by the infallible Church, was in itself sufficient guarantee for Vincent's good faith; but apart from this we have other evidence that he acted according to his conscience in his defense of Clement and his championship of the Avignon obedience. In 1389, he published the *Treaty of the Schism*. It contains two main propositions: first, no one should remain neutral, for government by two heads is a greater monstrosity than a two-headed man; therefore there is only one true pope. The only people in the world who have the right to indicate the true pope are the cardinals; they have declared Clement to be the true pope, therefore he must be so. Secondly, all the doctors of the Church declare that an election made under the constraint of fear is null and void.

This second proposition holds the key of the whole position. Catherine of Siena held that fear was not, in this particular case, a sufficiently dominating factor to invalidate the election, hence her support of Urban. Vincent, on the contrary, basing his decision on the reports of the cardinals, for he was not in personal touch with events in the same way as his Dominican sister, considered that fear had been the decisive factor in the election. Granted that his premise was correct, then he drew the right conclusion, and so in the circumstances, he did right in giving his obedience to Clement, as did France, Scotland and Castile.

The most powerful prop of the Avignon obedience was undoubtedly Pedro de Luna, Cardinal of Aragon. To him Vincent was bound in close ties of mutual admiration and friendship. This cardinal was, on many counts, worthy of the friendship of a saint. He was a man of exemplary moral character. Saint Antoninus speaks of him as a remarkable orator, while in qualities of heart he ceded to no one. Blancas says that if he had been the legitimate pope in happier times, his greatness of soul and high qualities of mind would have accomplished great things. But high position either makes or mars a man, and Pedro had other qualities of a far different order, qualities which might never have become apparent if he had remained only the Cardinal of Aragon, but which, after he had been elected Benedict XIII, became by degrees more and more apparent, blotting out his better qualities and leading to the deterioration of the whole man.

Fundamentally he was as obstinate as a mule, and self-love grew with his rising fortunes until it completely blinded him, suggesting to him a fund of more or less specious reasons for clinging to his own opinions, in opposition to everyone else, and to right reason also. So when, in 1394, Clement died and the Avignon cardinals elected Pedro as his successor, the new pontiff was placed in the one position above all others which would bring to prominence his undesirable qualities.

As soon as he had been elected pope, anxious to gather around him men who would reflect honor on his court, he chose among others the Friar Preacher whose name was already becoming widely known throughout Spain, Master

51

Vincent Ferrer. Benedict named him Papal Confessor as well as Penitentiary Apostolic and Master of the Sacred Palace. This gave the friar special opportunities to work for the ending of the schism, and he made use of his position to try to persuade his illustrious penitent to resign the papacy.

Already a past master of intrigue Benedict used every art of diplomacy. He temporized, promised under conditions which were not possible of fulfillment, did everything, in fact, except what was asked of him. He tried every means of bringing his confessor entirely to his own way of thinking; he even went so far as to attempt bribery, for Vincent was offered honors of all kinds, bishoprics, and a cardinal's hat. Smiling, the friar refused every honor, maintaining the sturdy independence which gave him right to freedom of speech, and this right he exercised fearlessly.

Whilst owning the obedience of Benedict the rulers of France strove by every means to obtain his resignation. In his brief intervals of sanity, the unfortunate Charles VI made personal appeals and sent ambassadors, as did both the Council and University of Paris; for by this time the pope of the Roman obedience, Urban, had died and had been followed by two successors, so that all hope of unity seemed farther off than ever. Finally, the French Marshal Boucicaut received orders to besiege Avignon in the hope that force of arms might effect what diplomacy was unable to accomplish.

But Pedro de Luna liked the din of battle, it afforded him an escape from thought, and just then he did not want to weigh too carefully these questions of right and wrong. Vincent, his confessor, could not approve his determination to fight; if he remained in the papal palace it would appear as if he were sanctioning it, and therefore he left and went to the priory of his own order in the town. For six months he continued preaching, praying for the Church and adding to his prayer penance of all kinds. But far more agonizing than any bodily penance was the torture of his soul; he suffered in the offense given to God, in the terrible ills from which the divided Church was suffering, and to this was added the personal grief of acting in opposition to the friend who loved and trusted him.

In 1398 the town was opened to the French army and the pontiff fell back on his fortified palace. Though Benedict placed the town under an interdict, Vincent continued to say Mass publicly. When we remember the intolerable strain which about this time brought him to death's door with fever, it is easy to understand how his tired, tortured brain might have led him to consider right an act which in itself was unlawful. But, just here, there is definite evidence showing that this apparent disobedience had no adverse effect on his influence with Benedict. Now Benedict, from all accounts, was extremely tenacious of his rights and dignity; therefore his continued friendship goes to prove that in some way he condoned Vincent's action in defying the interdict. From what we know of the tortuous diplomacy of the man, we may infer that it was not impossible that Vincent had his permission to disobey the interdict, though he was told to say nothing about it. Now Vincent was far too deeply revered and loved by the people for them to be critical of anything he might choose to do, and so there was no question raised about his saying Mass at this time. It was Master Vincent who did this thing and Master Vincent must be right!

Then, at last, the strain became too much even for his iron self-control, and Vincent fell ill of a fever so severe that he was brought to death's door.

On the third night of his illness, as he lay in the dormi-

53

tory, Saint Dominic, accompanied by Saint Francis of Assisi, appeared to comfort him. Then came Our Lord himself, in the midst of a great host of angels. Touching the sick man lovingly on the cheek, Our Lord bade him rise and preach throughout kingdoms and cities the approach of the Last Judgment. Vincent rose completely cured, and, loveliest of miracles, the mark of Our Lord's sacred fingers on his cheek remained with him for the rest of his life. This happened on the third of October, 1398.

The next day, Vincent made his way into Benedict's presence and told him of the command that Our Lord had laid on him. Benedict accepted the message as coming from God, but refused to allow Vincent to leave Avignon. Vincent knew that the voice of Christ's vicar is more assuredly the voice of Christ Himself than any vision could be, and as he firmly believed Benedict to be Christ's vicar the friar remained where he was until, on November 22nd, the pontiff sent him out to preach, armed with plenary powers and the title *Legatus a Latere Christi*.

It is beside the purpose of this book to follow step by step the progress of the schism: how Benedict escaped from Avignon and wandered the country, repudiated by most of those who had formerly owned his obedience; how with that strange magnetic power of his, he gradually won back to himself a larger following than ever. At times the end of the schism seemed in sight, at others, owing in great measure to the obstinacy and self-will of Benedict, all hope of reunion seemed indefinitely postponed. And so for eleven years the scandal dragged its weary way.

At last, in 1409, the cardinals themselves called a Council in Pisa and to it came eighty-four cardinals, two hundred bishops, four patriarchs, three hundred priests, the generals of all the great Religious Orders, deputies from the universities, and all the temporal rulers of the west, in fine all persons of importance under either obedience. The two pontiffs, Gregory XII of the Roman Obedience and Benedict XIII of the Avignon Obedience, were cited to appear before them; and when they did not come in response to the command, the Council condemned them for contumacy and decreed their deposition. They then proceeded to the election of a new pope.

No law, human or divine, can justify this action on the part of the cardinals and the other Fathers of the Council. One of the two pontiffs, Gregory or Benedict, was the true pope, the Head of the Church. It appertains to the pope alone to call a General Council and no other body can arrogate to itself the powers that belong to the pope alone. Moreover, this action, though it did, in the long run, bring about the end of the schism, at the time only succeeded in making the confusion still more inextricable; for now, instead of two, there were three claimants to the See of Peter. Ten months later, the newly elected antipope, Alexander V, died and John XXII was elected his successor. There was only one way out of the tangle; all three claimants must be persuaded to resign.

John XXII summoned a General Council to meet in Constance in 1414, and this Council demanded the resignation of all three pontiffs. John was the first to agree to this, and he was followed by Gregory who also agreed to resign if the others did likewise; there remained only Benedict. And as it is through Benedict that Vincent is vitally connected with the affair of the schism, it is necessary to shift the scene to Perpignan in Catalonia, close to the French border.

Benedict was in residence in his castle just beyond the city, and the King of Aragon, Ferdinand, a man sick almost to death, but determined, sick or well, to do all in his power to end the schism, was in residence in the town itself. From Perpignan the king sent to Saragossa where Vincent was preaching, begging him to come "in view of the good success of so important an affair in which the mediation of the faithful, and above all your prayers and advice are necessary."

In the meantime, the Emperor Sigismund, judging that the crucial point at the moment was focused at Perpignan rather than at Constance, left the Council and came as far as Navarre, in order to bring the pressure of his influence and unique position in Europe to bear in forcing a solution. Nearer than Navarre his dignity as Emperor did not permit his coming in person, so he sent ambassadors, giving strict injunctions that while treating Benedict with proper respect, they were not to show him the honors due to the pope.

But Vincent was doing more than either of these. Journeying back and forth many times between Perpignan and Navarre, he undertook the task of bringing about a rapport between emperor and pontiff, a task so delicate that one word capable of malinterpretation would throw the whole negotiation into confusion.

At last the emperor's ambassadors won from Benedict a promise that he would "do what was necessary for the good of the Church," and the emperor, who did not know the pontiff well enough to assess the true worth of such promises, took it at its face value and came in person to Perpignan. Once more all seemed about to end well, for Benedict even went so far as to receive ambassadors from the Council sitting at Constance.

Meanwhile Vincent, having at the moment no urgent and absorbing diplomatic duties, was preaching publicly in the town, converting Jews, Moors and Christian sinners by the hundred and—miracle of grace—the absorbing point of interest in the whole countryside became, not the progress of negotiations to end the schism, nor the illustrious visitors who thronged the town, but the humble Friar preaching penance. Perpignan, which had been as evil a spot as any garrison town, as any meeting place of the great, as any busy centre of wealth, commerce and luxury can be, now gave itself wholeheartedly to prayer and penance, while bands of flagellants made public reparation nightly for the vices which had been fostered there during the past months.

But Vincent himself could not forget, even for a moment, the terrible wound which scarred the Church; nor could he forget that the man whom he loved and revered, and whom he still held to be the true pope, was the only obstacle left in the path to reunion. Crowded days and consequent fatigue could not dispel nights of anguish, and at the end of a month, as once before at Avignon, he fell dangerously ill. The prior of the convent took the apparently dying man to his own cell for greater privacy, and Benedict sent his own physician to prescribe for him. Vincent said to the doctor:

"I thank the Sovereign Pontiff for his fatherly thought of me, and I thank you, too, for coming to see me, but you can do nothing. The Great Doctor has visited me today, telling me that I am to preach on Thursday. I can feel in myself that I am cured, and, since this is the work of God Himself, lesser physicians cannot touch me with their drugs."

The doctor left the cell saying, "According to human standards the friar has only an hour or two to live. But since he says he will preach on Thursday, preach he will."

As the friar had foretold, on Thursday morning he left the priory, went to the church, mounted the pulpit and, in the presence of the pontiff himself and a vast crowd, began

57

his sermon with a text from Ezechiel, which his hearers found terrifying in its strangeness.

*Ossa arida, audite verbum Dei.*—"Dry bones hear the word of God."

Benedict understood the text and the sermon which followed in all its implications; the listening crowd understood, for the preacher's meaning was unequivocal. Friar Vincent had won through his long agony, the divine Physician had brought light to his mind as well as healing to his body. In burning, blistering words he denounced the pontiff, whose obstinacy was the sole cause of the continuing schism.

Still the Emperor Sigismund did not despair of persuading Benedict to resign; perhaps he pinned more faith on the effect of Vincent's sermon than the friar did himself. In interview after interview he pressed home the matter of resignation until at last he drove the pontiff to formulate conditions under which, in Benedict's opinion, universal peace might be achieved:

"Let the Council of Constance be declared illegal and its decisions null and void, let a new one be summoned in France, in which, after he had been confirmed in his title as pope, he would lay down the tiara, but only on condition that he remained a cardinal, a legate *a latere*, with full juridical powers in the countries at present under his obedience."

Such an answer could be regarded as nothing short of mockery, and the infuriated emperor left the presence chamber to return to Constance. But in spite of his defiant words, Benedict had at last realized that the final move of the game had been played and that nothing remained for him but to disappear from public life with what dignity he could muster. Accordingly he left Perpignan at once for Colioure where his galleys were in harbor. From thence he sailed to the island of Peniscola off the Spanish coast where to the end he kept a shadow papacy in a shadow world. How far he honestly succeeded in deceiving himself we shall never know.

Meanwhile, King Ferdinand had summoned a Council of bishops and doctors, to whom were joined the ambassadors of Castille and Navarre, and the Counts of Armagnac and Foix, in other words, the remnants of those who had owned the Avignon obedience. The whole matter was now clear to all and it is this which gave the Council of Constance an authority which that of Pisa had lacked. Two pretenders to the papacy had resigned. Since the office of pope is that of Father, that man who like a true father preferred the good of Christendom to his own dignity was the true pope. John and Gregory had resigned into the hands of the Council, and so they had given the Fathers plenary power; Benedict, on the contrary, who refused to give up his position when the good of the Church demanded it, must, on that very count be a usurper.

According to Curits:

"Since Benedict could have given peace to the Church and refused to do so, in spite of all the prayers made to him, all the warning given him, it was right to withdraw from his obedience. By refusing to renounce it when the good of the Church required it, he had retained the Pontificate unjustly; therefore, it was necessary to treat him as if he had usurped that authority in the first place. If he were the true Father and Pastor, he would have preferred to see the Church united without him, rather than torn in two because of him, after the example of the mother in the judgment of King Solomon, who preferred to see her baby taken from her alive, rather than divided between her and the other claimant. After having listened to all these reasons, the King wished to hear what the venerable Master Vincent had to say. The holy man replied that, since Benedict had refused to listen to the third appeal, there were no more grounds for hesitation; for fresh delays would only add to the difficulties. If their obedience to him were not repudiated it would be impossible to hold the Council of Constance, because then all the cardinals and prelates under Benedict's obedience would naturally refuse to be present. Then the other obedience would proceed to an election which, in its turn, the Avignonese cardinals would repudiate as null and void; and thus the work of the Council would be useless and would simply perpetuate the schism.

" 'As for the pope,' he added, 'in my opinion it will be the man whom the cardinals elect. Only insist on an oath that all will be done according to God and conscience. If you demand further conditions, you run the risk of perpetuating disputes.' "

After careful deliberation of the matter, the Council decided to make a solemn repudiation of Benedict and to withdraw their allegiance. This Act of Renunciation was made on the Feast of the Epiphany, and Vincent Ferrer preached the preliminary sermon. He took as his text *They offered Him gifts,* and drew out the lesson by comparing the three princes—of Castile, Aragon and Navarre—to the three Magi, and the gifts they offered were the acts of Renunciation which gave peace to the Church.

After the sermon, Vincent read aloud the Act of Repudiation in the name of the King of Aragon. This repudiation couched in the same terms was published in Castile and Navarre at the same day and hour.

Although he was pressed to go to Constance for the

Council, although Alphonsus of Aragon in the name of his father and the theologian Gerson wrote to him begging him to attend, although the emperor sent messages in the same strain, Vincent did not go. The work which God had given him to do in regard to the schism was brought to a successful end, and now he knew that he must obey without longer waiting that other God-given command, to preach to all peoples and nations.

# part 2

# The Messenger of the Judgment

# Chapter VII

## *Legatus a Latere Christi*

With the first miraculous cure of Saint Vincent, the second part of his life begins. He was raised up by Our Lord Himself, and bidden to preach throughout the world the coming of the Last Judgment, and the healing hand of the Master renewed at one and the same time his bodily and spiritual powers. From now on there is not the slightest trace of that sensitive simplicity which, as in the case of the mason of Barcelona, led to its own undoing. There is exquisite tenderness of great charity, the sure instinct of soul given to one who loves God intensely, but from now on much of Vincent's personality is hidden behind the greatness of his mission.

Through the whole of western Europe he becomes a stupendous and portentous figure. Crowds listen to him for hours awestruck and enthralled. Kings, princes, bishops and town authorities seek his advice and follow his bidding. At one time or another the destinies of great tracts of France, Spain, Italy and the Alpine countries lie in his hands. He delivers his message in no uncertain terms, quite undismayed at its magnitude, and he confirms the message by miracles worked in circumstances of the utmost publicity. In all he says and does there is no trace of embarrassment, no fear of being misunderstood, apparently no fear of the greatest trial of the saints, the admiration and veneration of men.

Any consciousness of self seems non-existent in Vincent. If people choose to attribute to the man those things which simply pertain to his mission, the mistake is theirs, not his. As for him, Vincent, he is just the messenger of God, the messenger of the Judgment, *Legatus a Latere Christi*. Ambassadors of kings have a public mission, and as he is the ambassador of Christ, it stands to reason that he also must carry Credential Letters, set out in such a fashion that all may understand them. Later on he himself will explain his mission in detail. The first necessity is to find an answer to the question: what was the dignity and authority with which Benedict invested Vincent Ferrer when he gave the Saint permission to set out on his task of preaching through Europe, to begin a journey which was to end only with his death?

According to the Catholic Dictionary, a Legate a Latere Extraordinary is one deputed to visit foreign countries on extraordinary occasions, such as negotiations for a peace, or arrangements for a General Council. Vincent, then, as Ambassador Extraordinary of Christ Himself, and recognized as such by the pontiff whose obedience he owned, had authority to preach everywhere; no diocese, no city, no church could be closed to him. His powers of, and exemption from, jurisdiction were second only to those of the pope himself. A Friar Preacher is by his profession international; Vincent Ferrer's powers were international in the widest sense, both as to their scope and the extent of the country over which he exercised them. The length of his apostolate is almost unparalleled. Beginning at the age of fifty-one, invested by

God himself with almost limitless juridical powers, for eighteen years he tramped Europe on foot, until an open ulcer on his leg forced him to ride the little she-ass that became in her own sphere almost as well-known as her master.

The Europe of the present day with its battle scars, misery, hunger, disease, discontent, godlessness and vice is very like the Europe of Ferrer's days, and this is one reason why the saint's life should mean so much to our generation. France, still bleeding from the wounds of the first half of the Hundred Years War, was preparing for renewal of hostilities. Successive waves of plague—the Black Death—were sweeping the continent, a sad legacy of the crusades. Spain, Vincent's mother country, was overrun by Jews and Moors. Except in Granada, the Moors no longer ruled any part of the country; nevertheless, there was often trouble between them and their Christian neighbors. Still this was preferable to the state of those places where, to the great detriment of Christians, the Moors lived in close and peaceful proximity. For people whose powers of resistance were already weakened by recurrent plague and famine, whose grasp of religion was weak, and who were ill instructed, were an easy prey to proselytism.

Jews were then the moneyed, money-lending section of the community. Hating Christianity with fanatical hatred, they lost no opportunity of exploiting the needs of Christians to their own advantage. Then terrible, and in some cases, ungrounded tales of frightful deeds of cruelty attributed to the Jews would sweep through a city where they were already envied for their wealth, and hated for their use of it. People, maddened by fear and lusting for revenge, used to invade the ghettoes and massacre the inhabitants by the hundred.

Through this distracted land came a man, a Friar Preacher, no longer young, already an experienced public

**67**

preacher, a man accustomed to exercise the difficult role of intermediary between persons and states, the confessor of the pontiff and of more than one royal person. Even from a human standpoint, he was one whose influence was powerful.

He attacked the problem of the Jews first in its social aspect. A Jew is always a man apart; he is debarred from Christian food and he worships on another day of the week. Vincent advised the confinement of unconverted Jews in their ghettoes; behind those walls they were safe from the frenzied attacks of irresponsible elements among the population. As the Jews were gathered together it was easier to protect them, and Vincent did this more than once by going in person to the ghetto. In addition, the town magistrates had a check on the activities of the Jews; and tales of blasphemous mockeries of the Mass with massacred Christian children were too widespread and common to be entirely dismissed.

In one of his sermons the master shows how these restrictions also served for the conversion of the Jews:

*From the sermons; on the conversion of the Jews.* "You should note this and understand that adversity is the reason why so many Jews are converted to Christianity. This is why God has permitted these just and right laws to be carried out; as we read in Psalm LXXXII, *Fill their faces with shame; and they shall seek Thy name O Lord . . .* And although this authority is clear and sufficient, it is confirmed in Psalm LXXVII, *When He slew them, then they sought Him; and they returned and came to Him early in the morning.* And so the Jews are converted to God by tribulation and adversity; as Isaias says more clearly still: *Lord, they have sought after Thee in distress; in the tribulation of murmuring Thy instruction was with them;* that is, Thy instruction was accepted."

68

Having protected their persons, Vincent now proceeded to the salvation of their souls. He preached to them, held controversial meetings with the most learned of them, and converted them by the thousand. In 1391, he converted seven thousand Jews in Valencia alone, and ten thousand more throughout the kingdom. At Valladolid, a rabbi, famous for his erudition, was one of Vincent's hearers when he preached on the Law of Moses. Afterwards he publicly avowed that for the first time he understood the true interpretation of the Law of Moses. He was converted and baptized, receiving the name of Paul of Saint Mary because he came of the same tribe as the Blessed Virgin. Eventually he became a bishop, first of Carthegena, then of Burgos, and was instrumental in bringing many hundreds of his nation to the true faith.

The streets of towns and villages were full of prostitutes. Of them Vincent says in one of his sermons:

"The third defect of leprosy is that it is contagious; therefore the leper was segregated, and this signifies the sin of licentiousness, for one licentious person infects and corrupts another, just as one bad woman wishes all others to be like her. This applies to the self-constituted prostitute, who makes her living on the streets. . . . Do magistrates sin when they gather such women together in common brothels? Augustine says that if you segregate a prostitute from all intercourse with humanity, by which he refers to the licensed houses, you will disturb the whole place with her wickedness." *From the sermons; on prostitution.*

He showed the magistrates how to carry out this advice. First, they built special quarters in the town surrounded by walls in which quarter all prostitutes were obliged to live.

69

This brought them into touch with humanity, for they were no longer outlaws, but were under rule like other citizens. Next Vincent forbade their leaving their quarters during Holy Week, the magistrates agreeing to pay them a living wage during that period. Finally, at Valencia in 1390 Vincent spent the last three days with them, giving them, as we should say, a retreat. The result was a mass conversion of such efficacy that many men of the city asked for the hands of these penitents in honorable marriage, and because the girls were poor the magistrates gave them sufficient for dowries. What Vincent initiated in Valencia he also carried out in many other large places.

At the other end of the social scale we find his royal penitent Queen Yolande, wife of John I. The tact and unbreakable firmness of Vincent's direction so transformed an imperious, irascible woman as to bring her at last to ask pardon of a member of her suite with whom she had been impatient.

She had lessons too in curbing curiosity, for, hearing of the ecstasies of her confessor, Yolande would not rest content until she had seen him at prayer surrounded by celestial light. Knowing that nothing would induce Vincent to permit her to visit his cell, she so wrought on his socius that at last he took her to the forbidden precincts of the dormitory and threw the cell door open. There the friar knelt on the floor in the middle of the room. Everyone else saw him but to the queen he was invisible. Vincent's companion was considerably perturbed, for the queen was saying aloud that she could see no one; and the brother knew by hearsay of the violence of her temper. So he walked rather nervously up to Vincent.

"The queen is here," he whispered, pulling him by the sleeve. Without moving, gravely, the friar replied:

"Do you not know that it is forbidden for women to enter our cells?"

The queen could hear the voice easily though she could see no one. All agog, half angry, half thrilled at the prodigy, she called out:

"Father, where are you?"

Again the grave voice of rebuke: "I am here, hidden from your sight. Go now. And learn that if you had been actuated by any worse motive than mere feminine levity, God would have punished you severely."

The queen had no option but to leave the cell, her curiosity ungratified for the time. However, she was a determined woman and by no means lacking in courage, so she applied to the prior who agreed to send for her at a propitious moment. She came with a large suite and this time, since it was at the invitation of the prior, she saw the saint kneeling in ecstasy, surrounded by a nimbus of light which, shining from his own person, filled the whole room. Vincent was quite unaware of her presence, and so impressed was she that she never afterwards addressed him except on her knees.

Such was Vincent as he appeared to others, strong, virile, and diffusing vitality, a philosopher and a theologian, a man with highly developed speculative intellect and yet at the same time eminently practical, a man accustomed to deal successfully with any situation, however complicated, a man of vast mind and a man of affairs. But what was the source from which this super-man drew his strength? The manner of life observed by this apostle throughout his journeyings gives the answer.

He rose at two o'clock and said Matins chorally, in choir if he were in one of his priories, otherwise with the companions of his journeys. This was followed by the entire psalter, after which he read the sacred Scriptures, remaining absorbed in God until the fire of his prayer drove him to the discipline. Each morning he went to confession. At six o'clock in the summer, and at seven in winter he sang Mass. This was followed by a sermon generally lasting three hours, after which he healed the sick and reconciled those at enmity with each other. Merely to read the contemporary epitomes of his sermons explains how the saint held a mixed audience spellbound for three hours on end.

At one o'clock he broke his fast on soup, fish, and wine well-watered. Nothing would induce him to eat more. At half-past one he said the Day Hours and then occupied himself with the poor, children, country-folk, and lastly with his own following. Then, if he were on a journey, he made a start for the next halting place.

At eight o'clock he retired to say his Office—Vespers and Compline—and to prepare his sermon for the next day. At nine o'clock, he lay down on the floor or the bare ground, placed his Bible or a stone for a pillow, and took his rest. Only in his last illness did he lie on a bed.

Resplendent among the virtues of this great soul shone patience. Picture his days, one endless march. Picture hunger, thirst, heat and cold, weariness, gales and tempests, rain, snow and burning sun; picture the difficulties of the roads which at their best would now-a-days be considered no more than mere tracks. On foot, or on the back of his little donkey, he traversed western Europe four times in fifteen years, preaching at least once every day, more often twice. Picture the places where he was often forced to spend the night, the dirty, half barbarous villages, the insanitary hovels, remembering at the same time that in the Middle Ages sanitation was confined to the monasteries.

Imagine the crowds who thronged and jostled him day

72

after day. Imagine the sick and those with suppurating wounds. Imagine the cow-herd from his byre, the leather dresser, the muddy peasant from the field. Imagine the dirty hands pawing the wonder-worker, the kisses which were rained on his hands and clothes, the pieces torn off his habit and scapular until the friar looked more like a scarecrow than a famous preacher. Imagine the daily hours when he gave himself to the poor and sick to listen, to bless, to cure. Imagine all this and then say whether pride, or weariness and nausea were the enemies he had to fight. And since it may be suggested that a fifteenth century man is being given a twentieth century temperament, here is an extract from one of Vincent's sermons on the coming of the Last Day which surely carries behind it hours of patient suffering.

"The second matter with regard to the judgment is the preparation of the place. . . . Therefore the place must be got ready; for, if a king was obliged to hold his court in a dwelling used by pigs and cattle, that dwelling must be cleansed and purified. The same holds good with regard to this world in which dwell beasts of burden. Those who live according to reason are men; those who follow their senses are beasts; the proud are lions; the avaricious foxes; the sensual pigs; the envious dogs; the greedy are wolves; the angry snakes or vipers; the lazy donkeys. Therefore the house of this world is corrupt, unclean and infected. . . . Therefore it must be cleansed and purified and this purification must be by fire which is kindled and fanned to the four parts of the world in the east and west, and burns the whole world. . . . After this Christ comes to judgment, with His Mother, the Virgin Mary, and the lords and soldiers of heaven. If the world were not purified, perchance the Virgin Mary would say to her Son: *From the sermons; on the last judgment.*

**73**

" 'O my Son! Why have you brought me into such a disgusting place?'

"If you say to me:

" 'O Brother! We do not perceive any unpleasantness.' Neither do the fish perceive the bitterness of the salt water because they have been born and bred there. The ostler does not perceive the stench of his stable, but the soldier who goes in notices it. So we do not notice the foulness of this world because we have been born and bred in this ill-savored place. But let only one blessed soul come from paradise and he will be quick to notice it."

Was there any reward even in this world for a life of virginal chastity, heroic labor and unquenchable love of God and souls? A witness at Vincent's canonization—one among many—says: "When travelling Vincent often leaned on me when going up or down steps and always, at the touch of his hands, he exhaled a marvellously sweet odor which lasted with me for three or four days. This experience, several times repeated, did not permit of any doubt in this respect."

# Chapter VIII

## *The Disciples of Friar Vincent*

In his character as Legate of Christ Vincent Ferrer travelled through Spain, Northern Italy, the Alpine countries, South Germany and France, and in every city, town or village that he visited he encountered the same difficulties. There were places where the inhabitants were frankly pagan, sun worshippers or even worse. Elsewhere the majority of the folk knew little or nothing of their professed religion. Many could not say the *Pater* correctly, more still were unable to make the Sign of the Cross.

Peter d'Ailly wrote: "Priests no longer know the law, princes no longer possess justice, nor old men wisdom; people have the faith no longer, nor have children respect for those in authority. Subjects no longer love their masters. Prelates have no religion, neither have monks devotion, nor nuns honor. There is no discipline among the young, doctrine among the clerics, learning among masters, respect among students, justice among servants, integrity among judges, fidelity among soldiers. There is no concord among citizens, fellowship among peasants, integrity among workmen, truth among merchants, generosity among the rich, chastity among virgins, no virtue nor mourning among widows, no continence nor fidelity among married couples. Now, brethren, can such a state of things exist unless Antichrist has come; since Christ has no standing and is regarded as a stranger and wanderer among the powerful of this world?"

Vincent himself says much the same:

*From the sermons; on the presence of Antichrist.*  "Where today may you find religious who realize their breaches of rule, vows, or ceremonies? Where can you find devoted clerics who are chaste and honorable? Where will you find prelates who have more care for souls than for revenues? Where are there conscientious temporal lords, and soldiers content with their pay? Where are there just lawyers, straightforward merchants, without fraud, usury or crooked dealing? Where are the farmers who pay their tithes? Where are there good and honorable women? They all wish to be called good and honorable, but their vanity shews them to be the very opposite."

In every town and village where the friar preached conversions were numbered by the thousand; and the majority were real and lasting. Feuds were brought to an end, enemies reconciled, harlots were cleared from the streets, priests returned to the care of their flocks, and people began to serve God in earnest. As a result of this, in every place that the friar visited, there were many who decided to follow him for a longer or shorter time. They were hungry to expiate their sins and to receive further instruction to strengthen them against a relapse.

Thus Vincent was always followed by a band three or four thousand strong, varying in its components from town to town as fresh penitents joined and others returned to their ordinary trades. But from among this great shifting crowd was gradually formed a nucleus of disciples who left all things to follow Christ and His apostle. This stable band of followers whose number varied from one hundred and fifty to three hundred was extraordinarily varied in its composition. There were monks, friars and secular priests who had obtained permission to share in Vincent's apostolate. Among them was at least one Carthusian who was allowed to join while retaining his status as a Carthusian. These ministered to the newly converted, heard confessions and gave instructions. Some were left behind to complete the work of reform in different places where the Friar preached, rejoining the main body later.

Besides these clerics there was also a band of lay-folk, both men and women. The majority of these were either converted sinners or those whose hearts had been smitten with grief for the sins of the world. These men and women were irresistibly drawn to expiate their own sins or those of others, souls truly and deeply wounded by the arrow of divine Love. An outlet was necessary and they sought that outlet consecrated by the usage of their own time.

All through the ages, conversion is only another name for penance, and each century turns to penance of a different kind. The first centuries produced the hermits of the Thebaid, who were followed by cenobites leading a common life of almost superhuman rigor. Monastic segregation was followed by the mendicancy of the friars, and all through these ages, ordinary folk expiated public sins by public penance. It was part of the scheme of things.

During the thirteenth and fourteenth centuries, time and again, confraternities of flagellants were formed by men who were hungry to show their gratitude to God for the grace of repentance, and their hatred of sin as an offense against His Majesty. Sooner or later such confraternities lost their right spiritual poise, penance became the end instead of a means to the end of union with God by charity, and then they had to be suppressed. But even so, they were a natural reaction of that time to the problems of sin and repentance, and so, almost immediately, Friar Vincent's followers formed themselves into a band of flagellants.

The saint had no illusions either as to the powerful instrument for good that he had in such a confraternity, nor of the dangers that might arise therefrom. Public penance of this kind, uncontrolled, might easily lose its high original purpose in unwholesome excitement; then vicious evils would necessarily follow, sadism and sex perversion. So Vincent, in his God-given wisdom, placed the one safe curb on this fiery impulse for good, by regulating it all by obedience.

The master instituted a rule for his disciples and gave them a habit. Before they were even admitted as aspirants they were subjected to a rigorous examination. The master insisted that they must be free from every obligation, such as dependent parents, and they must also be free from debt. If they were married there was to be a mutual pact of separation, while wealthy people had to distribute their goods to the poor. It is more than probable that the master also insisted on their obtaining permission from the bishop of their diocese. In spite of the nomadic life they led, they followed a rule of life as strict as that of any cloister. Though these penitents made no religious vows, they were obliged to submit to a period of testing—a novitiate—as strict as that of any monastic house.

To each was assigned certain tasks, either for the spiritual or material welfare of the rest, or in assisting their hosts at the different places where the party stopped. Liturgical Office was recited publicly; every day there was Solemn High Mass, generally sung in the open, for no church could contain the crowds who flocked to hear Master Vincent, and they formed the choir.

The processions of the discipline were also carried out strictly in accordance with rule, and not as the attraction or devotion of the individual might lead him. The processions were formed up at the entrance to places where the master was going to preach; when practicable the time chosen was dusk, and the habits were made so that a decent baring of the shoulders alone was possible. There was, therefore, not much risk in the performance of a penance, in itself unpleasant, strictly in accordance with the routine of rule.

Father Vincent's disciples were strictly forbidden to beg; in fact, on more than one occasion, he publicly warned his listeners against any persons who asked for charity in his name; they were all, he said, imposters. But there was no lack of spontaneous charity on the part of the people whose towns the friar visited, and God, never behind in generosity, often caused the miraculous multiplication of provisions. In many cases the friar came at the express invitation of the magistrates of the place, and then hospitality and honor demanded that they should see to it that there was a sufficiency of food.

There was a properly constituted hierarchy among Vincent's disciples; certain monks, friars and priests were put in charge of different groups and each contingent owed obedience to its leader. Added to this was the enormous prestige of Vincent himself. All loved him, but they must have stood greatly in awe of a man whose preaching was so evidently inspired by God and whose gift of reading hearts was clearly miraculous. Often enough it happened that during a sermon someone in the crowd would throw on to the platform a folded piece of paper with a question. On the following day the question would be answered in every detail, but the piece of paper would still be lying where it had been thrown. The most hardy would think twice before doing anything of which he would be ashamed before those kindly, piercing dark eyes.

Finally we come to what must have been the source of gravest difficulty to those in charge of the band, and where the friar's immense powers of control and organization were shown most brilliantly; I refer to the large group of women. There is no difficulty in dealing with any woman who has been able to mould her life in accordance with her God-given nature. She is essentially a mother in that she demands opportunity to give love, nurture, service, and herself. The married woman in her home, the unmarried woman occupied in a direction which is consonant with her nature, either in schools, hospitals, orphanages, nursing or caring for the sick, aged, poor and friendless—in a word, in the service of the needy—fit perfectly into the scheme of things. An enclosed nun only fulfils her primary obligation as a woman in so far as she expends herself in prayer for the world. But when a woman is occupied in work having no relation to life, or where her sphere of work does not allow her sufficient scope, then her God-given instincts run riot and she is a scourge both to herself and to others. For she seeks, in excitement and desire for notice, what her nature rightly demands of her as sacrifice. So she becomes perverted, self-seeking, bad, greedy.

In that multitude of women who followed the saint there must have been all the material for a fine series of scandals; and the fact that during the whole time that they followed him not one whisper of scandal was breathed shows both his wisdom in dealing with them and their awe of his sanctity.

These women were of every social class and kind. There was the converted harlot, the penitent worldling and the fundamentally good, and these must have presented comparatively little difficulty; the potential source of trouble would have been the pious little person whose great ambition in life was to look after the dear fathers. Vincent himself remarked that, though he could not drive them away, he had never desired nor asked the women to come.

Since they were there, however, sound common sense dealt with the situation. The women travelled in a group apart. The mother instinct was given an outlet in that they saw to the material welfare of the rest. They were thus given what was needful for their peace of mind, but selfishness and indulgence of romantic pettiness had little scope in that they cooked and mended for the rest of the community as a body. There must have been untold joy, though plenty of physical weariness in cooking for thousands, and mending hundreds of torn habits and worn-out sandals. One can imagine them saying with satisfaction: "What a joy it is to do all this for the poor tired hungry dears." But there was no chance of murmuring with smug satisfaction: "There! I have put a piece of something extra in Fray Pedro's soup, and I hope he will guess it was I who did it for him."

Thus it was that all those, both men and women, who followed Vincent simply in order to serve God better were amply satisfied with the result of their venture, while those who merely came for love of excitement, novelty, or notice soon dropped off. Sooner or later, however, nomadic life came to an end, even for those who persevered; many joined only for a stated length of time, others were left behind in small groups to leaven the communities of convents and monasteries that the friar had reformed. In at least one case, a new convent was founded in which Vincent placed the whole group of women who happened to be following him at the time.

And so all was as it should be. Having led men to God, Vincent left them with God, and himself went forward on the never-ending journey to which he had been called.

# Chapter IX

## *One of the Journeys of Master Vincent*

It was in October 1398 that Vincent received from Our Lord his divine mission and title *Legatus a Latere Christi,* but for a time Benedict would not free him from the papal court so that he might go where the Spirit of God should lead him. Vincent, ever obedient, waited on at Avignon, and the pontiff went so far as to relieve him of his charge as papal confessor and to permit him to make preaching excursions in Catalonia. He also sent him on various diplomatic missions, among others to the King, Don Martin.

At last, more than a year later, on November 22, 1399, Benedict gave the friar formal permission to depart, endowing him with plenary powers, that is, he gave him the power to bind and loose, even in those cases usually reserved for the Holy See. And so begins the unending journey of which a contemporary author says: "Every step was a miracle, every word a victory for heaven."

The point of his departure was Carpentras, the chief town in Venaissin. The province was a stronghold of the obedience of Benedict, and so it was a fitting starting point. There he was received with the greatest honor, the magistrates vying with one another to show him respect. His own brethren showed their satisfaction at his presence in a banquet for which they purchased a monster sole costing six liards.

After some months spent in the Midi, the saint turned his steps in the direction of Dauphiné, Savoy and the Alpine valleys. These countries were a stronghold of the Vaudois who by their pseudo-mysticism had utterly deceived and subjugated the simple mountaineers. An extant letter from Vincent to his master general, John de Puynoix, gives an account of this apostolate.

*Letter to his master general, John de Puynoix; from the text of Honorius Bouche in his History of Provence.*

"Very Reverend Father and Master,

"Because of my innumerable occupations I have not yet been able to write to your Paternity as I ought. The fact of the matter is that since you left Romans, until today, I have been obliged to chant Solemn Mass daily, to preach twice or three times, so that little time was left me for such matters as eating or sleeping; and even now I have to prepare my sermons while travelling. But, so that you may not impute my silence to negligence or want of respect, I have, for several weeks now, snatched a few minutes daily from my ordinary work to let you know, at least, the way by which I am travelling.

"After your departure from Romans, I preached for three or four consecutive months in Dauphiné, travelling through the towns and villages which I had not already visited, and returning to the too-famous valleys of the diocese of Embrum which are packed with heresy. One is named Lucerne, another Argentière and the third Valpure—The Pure Valley —originally the worst of the lot. I have already passed

84

through them several times, and they have listened to Catholic doctrine with respect, but I judged it wise to pass through them again to confirm them in their good will.

"I have been asked several times, both by word of mouth and in writing, to go into Lombardy. I have preached there for thirteen months partly in the countries under your obedience and also farther afield, for example, in the domain of the Marquis of Montferrat, since I was unable to refuse his pressing invitation. I then crossed the mountains and found there also many valleys infested by Vaudois and Cathari.

"Afterwards I travelled through the diocese of Turin, visiting each locality in turn, and in each place preaching Catholic truths in refutation of the errors into which these good folk had fallen.

"Thanks be to God! They received the true doctrine eagerly and with the most touching respect, Our Lord cooperating with my words and deigning to confirm them. (He does not add "by miracles" though this is obviously his meaning.)

"It is plain to me that all these errors and heresies result in great part from the lack of preachers. For thirty years now no missionary has been amongst them except for the Vaudois heretics who come from Aquiles twice a year. So, Venerable Master, you will see what a weight of responsibility rests on the prelates and on all those who are bound by their office to the work of preaching. I grieve to say that these men prefer to live in the large towns where they have fine apartments, filled with every comfort, while souls for whom Jesus Christ died are perishing without them. They are dying for want of spiritual nourishment, and there is no one to break the Bread of Life to the children; the

harvest is abundant but the laborers are very few. I pray the
Lord of the harvest to send laborers to His vineyard.

"Concerning the heretic bishop whom I found in one of
these valleys called Loforio, I must tell you that he wished
to speak with me, and that he is now converted. I may say
as much of the Vaudois schools in the Engroya valley; the
schools no longer exist. The Cathari of Valpoint have renounced their abominable superstitions. The heretics of the
valley of Quinti, where the murderers of Blessed Peter Martyr found refuge, have received me well; factions have
ceased, the Guelphs and Ghibellines have signed a pact of
peace; treaties of allegiance have also been signed. As for
other matters too difficult to enumerate, which God has
deigned to operate for His glory and the good of souls, I
will say nothing for the moment except that they have been
blessed in every way.

"After passing thirteen months in Lombardy, I entered
Savoy five months ago at the repeated requests of the
bishops and temporal lords of the country. I have been
greatly interested in visiting the four dioceses of Sion, Taren-
taise, Maurienne and Grenoble, preaching in the surrounding country according to the needs of the moment. Now I
am here in Geneva.

"Among the monstrous errors which infest the country of
Geneva, there is one which consists in rendering public cultus
to a sort of divinity whom they call Saint Orient, that is to
say, the sun. This cult is very widespread, it has its confraternities and its principal feast is on the day after Corpus
Christi. Parish priests and religious have told me that they
dare not preach, nor even speak in public against this error,
because the sectaries threaten them with death, and meanwhile prevent their receiving the wherewithal to live. By
dint of preaching daily and insisting on the heinousness of

idolatry, thanks be to God, and the support that He has given to my word, this error has at last entirely disappeared and the poor folk are now distressed beyond measure at having erred so gravely in such a fundamental matter of faith.

"I am preparing to visit the diocese of Lausanne, another place where the sun is publicly adored, above all in the country places. If the bishop, who has come twice or thrice to beg me to go there, is to be believed, there are on the confines of Germany and Savoy whole towns entirely peopled by heretics. I have been warned that these heretics are particularly dangerous; but I put my trust in God's unfailing mercy, and so I am going there this coming Lent. May the will of God be done everywhere as it is in heaven!

"My socius, Brother Antony, and I recommend ourselves humbly to your Paternity. May the Son of the Virgin Mary preserve you for a long time for the example and safeguard of our holy institutions,

"Your humble child and a useless servant of Christ,
"Friar Vincent Ferrer, Preacher.
"Finished at last and signed at Geneva, November 17, 1403."

There were, therefore, two classes of unbelievers with whom Vincent had to deal: the Vaudois or Cathari, who taught that neither priesthood, sacraments nor sacramentals were of the slightest use towards salvation, claiming that their own unauthorized preaching and the witness of their pseudo-mortified lives should take their place; the others were pagans pure and simple.

In the impure valley, which Vincent rechristened The Pure Valley, these fanatics made more than one attempt on the preacher's life. One night, armed with swords and knives, they climbed the roof of the friar's lodging and would have killed him if God had not protected him.

Penitents converted by Vincent tolerated no half measures in their repentance. Numbers of penitent Albigensians, Vaudois, sun-worshippers and others of vicious life sought the Chartreuse near Grenoble and the Carthusian habit in which to expiate their sins. The Carthusian General at the time was Vincent's brother, Bernard. One brother preached penance while the other offered the means of penance. "I received sometimes as many as five on one day," Bernard writes. Vincent himself visited the monastery more than once.

It was about this time that he met Bernardine of Siena, then a young man. The future Franciscan was travelling through Northern Italy seeking a career. He heard the saint preach and saw the future which God had intended for him. Vincent, for his part, was attracted to this youth, and invited him more than once to share his austere meal. One day after Bernardine had joined the Franciscans, Vincent said of him:

"Give thanks to God for this young man and for your country; he will be the honor of the religious of the blessed poor Man of Assisi; I am leaving him the task of evangelizing lovely Italy. He has a future before him; I am getting old, but the designs of God have their hour; he will be among the saints before I am." In point of fact, Saint Bernardine was canonized five years before Saint Vincent.

During this journey Vincent met Margaret of Savoy, then still a child of innocent and austere life. Later she married the Marquis of Montferrat, but as long as he lived Vincent never lost sight of her and even after his death he continued his protection; Margaret is one of the beatified members of the Dominican Order.

All through his life, Vincent appears to have been an object of pious curiosity; well for us that it was so. Friar Theobald, a member of the community of the Priory at Alba, where Vincent made a stay while in the neighborhood, gave his cell up to the use of the illustrious visitor. However, he possessed a second key, though he kept both the fact and the key to himself, for he wanted to go into the cell unnoticed as often as it seemed good to him. In fact, he availed himself to the full of his opportunities. One night he went in unnoticed; the next night he repeated his visit twice, following the same procedure for a third night. Then growing more and more interested and curious he began to slip in at all hours. Always he found Master Vincent reading or praying, sometimes speaking to God as if His divine Majesty were visibly present before him.

The path of the saint was, as always, strewn with miracles. At Ferusasco, where he preached, a poor woman brought him her child who was suffering from epilepsy. At the touch of the preacher the disease entirely disappeared, nor was there ever any recurrence.

At Montecalieri, the man who gave him hospitality, asked him:

"Master, what can I do to be delivered from the storms which, year after year, devastate the countryside?"

"For this year," replied the saint, "I will see to it."

Some time later a terrific storm broke, followed by hail which changed fields of promising crops into a veritable desert. But in the midst of this desolate expanse, lay the undamaged cornlands of Vincent's benefactor like a green island in a sombre lake.

"You do not realize," the saint was accustomed to say, "what potent means the Church puts at your disposal; use holy water with faith and your land will be safe." His hearers derided him, but when they saw one disastrous storm succeed another, the villagers came to him, contrite and humble, to implore his help. The saint showed no annoyance.

"Have no fear, my good fellows," he said, "God will come to your help."

Under his hand of blessing the fields of grain flourished, and never before had the farmers reaped such a magnificent harvest.

Holy water played a large part in his ministrations. One day he was exorcising a possessed person with what was supposed to be holy water, but with no result. On the contrary the devil cried out:

"What good water! Truly this is good water!"

The saint made the Sign of the Cross over the water, and the devil was immediately put to flight.

We find in the master's sermons more evidence about what he found in Lombardy. We read in one of those which were epitomized:

*From the sermons (one that is epitomized); on findings in Normandy.*

"Master Vincent says that he was grieved at finding in Lombardy nine valleys full of heretics, and this because of the small number of preachers. In one of these valleys, the people told him: 'Brother, for the last thirty years no brother has come here, nor any other priest to instruct us in our faith. But heretics come from distant places and preach their errors to us, and so we fall into heresy which we might have avoided if we had been taught the gospel doctrine.' This Jeremiah foresaw when he said: 'The little ones—that is the country folk, the ignorant, and the heretics—have asked for bread—that is the gospel teaching—and there was none to break it unto them.'"

90

In another sermon we learn how he discovered by practical experience the ways in which the heretical teachers deceived the poor folk of the valleys.

"Master Vincent wished to know in what ways these heretics deceived those others who before had been good Christians. And he understood that these teachers came in the clothing of sheep, as ascetics living on nothing but bread and water. Then, when they had gained the reputation of saints, the heretics asked their dupes: 'Do people in this country go to confession?' 'Yes,' they were told. 'To whom?' was the next question. 'To priests and religious,' answered the simple folk. Then said they: 'Why to priests and religious more than to others?' And they persuaded them that they ought not to confess to priests, because, they said, Christ did not restrict confession to priests only. And they quoted from the Epistle of Saint James: *Confess therefore your sins one to another; and pray for one another, that you may be saved.*

*From the sermons (one that is epitomized); on heretical teachers.*

" 'Now, is it not better,' say they, 'to confess to good secular persons than to bad priests, since such cannot loose that which is bound?'

"O traitors! This is what they say and affirm against the teaching and determination of the Catholic Church; for Christ with His own mouth said that it pertained to priests only to hear Confessions. To priests only has Christ committed the power of absolution, saying: *Whose sins you shall forgive they are forgiven, and whose sins you shall retain they are retained.*

"He said to the lepers who were figures of sin: *Go show yourselves to the priests,* because, although they may be evil in themselves, they only hold the Keys.

"Again these heretics were accustomed to say that the

91

people should not go to church, where there were idols—
that is statues—neither should they pray there in preference
to any other place, since God is everywhere. In fact, it was
better to pray in the fields and such places. Also they said
that people should not go to Mass.

"It will be even so in the time of Antichrist when his
messengers come. And first there will be demons in the
clothing of sheep; for there were some of these who came to
Master Vincent in the form of hermits, and told him that
the Sabbath and not the Sunday should be observed as a
holy day. So, as Christ said, *By their fruits ye shall know
them.*"

It was in Lombardy too that the devil succeeded in raising a fresh storm against the preacher. In different parts
of the country there lived certain mysterious hermits; these
men had great influence, each one in his own neighborhood,
over the simple country folk, earnest and anxious to do
right, but credulous, and too simple to be able to distinguish true doctrine from false. No one knew whence these
men had come, nor on what they lived, so strange were
they. The country folk regarded them with superstitious
fear and gave great heed to all their exhortations. Before
the arrival of Vincent they gathered the people together in
the public places and warned them against the preacher
who was coming in their midst, and of whom so much was
heard.

"We know," they said, "that this man is an imposter.
We have been told so in revelation." The devil was busy
sowing tares.

So, when Vincent came to any village in the vicinity of
one of these strange hermitages, in spite of the renown of
his preaching and his miracles, he was coldly received.

"We know who you are," they told him, "and that you are only trying to deceive the people. An old hermit in whom we have great confidence has warned us to have nothing to do with you. And the proof he has given us of your wickedness is that you follow the false pope who is Antichrist."

But such failures were few and far between; in general, Vincent was received with the greatest honor. When he reached Friburg on Saturday, March 5, 1404, all the bells in the city were rung for joy and the magistrates came out in a body to welcome him and present him with "the wine of honor." Innumerable crowds gathered to greet him, so that soldiers had to patrol the streets to prevent any disorders. All the expenses of the visit were defrayed by the public purse. The saint preached there for five days beginning on the fourth Sunday of Lent.

In the diocese of Bellay the saint gained another faithful disciple, one moreover who has proved of inestimable service to the biographers of the saint, since his deposition at the saint's canonization contains details which are not found elsewhere. At the Chartreuse of Notre Dame de Pierre Chatel a young monk, John Placentis, had not long been professed. The saint preached outside the Chartreuse to the crowds who followed him everywhere; he also preached to the monks inside.

John was so struck with Vincent's extraordinary gift for reading consciences that he asked and obtained permission to follow the saint, without ceasing to be a Carthusian, a strong proof of the austerity of the lives of Vincent's followers. For several years he went everywhere with the preacher, from time to time making a longer or shorter stay at a monastery of his own Order, chiefly that he might have the opportunity of committing to writing what he him-

self knew of the man who would, he was sure, be sooner
or later raised to the altars of the Church.

A letter written to the bishop by the magistrates of Orihuela in 1411 will not be out of place here, giving as it does
a picture of what happened in every place that the saint
visited.

"Very Reverend Father and Lord, we believe that your
Reverence will be pleased to know that Brother Vincent,
Master in Theology, has come into your diocese, has visited
Alicante, Elche, Orihuela, Murcia, and that he is now at
Lorca. His presence has produced immense good in the
whole country, particularly in this town. Thanks be to God
and to Master Vincent's preaching, there are now no longer
vices and public sins among us. For example: no one, little
or great, dares any longer to swear by the Name of God,
nor of the Virgin Mary, nor by the Blood of Christ, nor the
like. If anyone is surprised into blasphemy he makes good
and prompt reparation. All gaming houses are shut, and we
have renounced our privilege in this respect. Neither dice
nor any other dangerous games of the kind are in use. There
are no more conspiracies, magic practices nor cabalistic
signs. No one goes now to consult fortune tellers nor sorcerers; priests no longer play games of chance as they used to
do and immoral feasts have been suppressed. Fraternal correction keeps vice at a distance.

"People have never been to their duties as they are going
at present. Our priests are not sufficiently numerous to hear
Confessions and give Holy Communion. On Sundays and
Feasts of Devotion, everyone, men, women and children,
except infants, come to Mass with a devotion which must be
seen to be believed. The churches used to be too big, now
they are too small. In a word, my Lord, we can affirm this

of every place through which the friar passes. May God be praised! And you likewise, my Lord, because we owe the visit of Master Vincent to you. May God preserve him for a long time in grace, and at his death place him among the apostles, martyrs and confessors.

"One of the great favors he has obtained for us is that there is no longer plague, pestilence, or discord. All in good will and for the love of Our Lord have mutually pardoned all offenses. We have counted one hundred and twenty-five reconciliations, twenty-five are of blood feuds, and the rest follow maiming. May God be blessed for such a peace. Only two, the priest, John Flavia, and a newly converted Christian, have refused to be reconciled, and the people are not a little scandalized to see a priest thus refuse to pardon. We pray then for the preservation of Master Vincent in return for so many benefits, and for you also who persuaded him to come. May the Lord keep you for a long time in His holy Service. Given at Orihuela, March 14, 1411."

Vincent's ministry in the Alpine countries ended when he was recalled to Lyons by Master John Goutel, armed with a letter from the directorate, and the chapter of the great church of which he was titular Lector.

# Chapter X

## *The Messenger of the Judgment*

When, as we have already seen, on the night of October 3rd Vincent lay sick to death, broken under the weight of the Great Schism, he was visited by Our Lord in company with Saint Dominic and Saint Francis. The reason given for the miraculous cure which followed was that he was to preach the approaching end of the world and the Last Judgment.

This brings us to the crucial point of our saint's life, his right to the title of angel—in the sense of messenger—of the Judgment, and the authenticity of the message which he declared himself divinely appointed to deliver to the world. Not once, but many times, he repeats in different words this message; we meet in his sermons such warnings as:

*(Through page 98)*
*From the sermons;*
*on the last judg-*
*ment.*
"*Nox praecessit, dies autem appropinquavit.* This text, and indeed the whole epistle, assures us of the fact that the end of the world is near, in order that we may place in it neither our love nor our hope. For, unless he be a fool, no man who is aware that his house is old and threatens to fall

in ruins, wishes to continue occupying it. . . . In the same way, the house of this world is ancient and ruinous, so that no one but a fool will desire or choose it."

Or on the text:

*"Go into the city—which is heaven—that is over against you.* Now I am going to explain how we ought to enter and take possession of paradise and eternal life. And it is proper to do so for, as you learnt in yesterday's sermon, since the world is to end so shortly, it is right that you should know how we may attain eternal life of which there is no end."

The first question which rises to the mind is that it is now over five hundred years since Vincent delivered his message and the end is not yet. Was he deceived? Since time is nothing else but movement, the extent or duration of time can only be measured by comparison with other periods of time. Now, even these five hundred years, to us with our seventy or eighty years span of life, an exceedingly long time, are in reality exceedingly short in comparison with the hundreds of thousands of years which have elapsed since God said: *Let there be light, and light was made. . . . And there was evening and morning one day.*

It is certain that we are in the last age of the world; we have Scripture warrant for it. *Amen I say to you that this generation shall not pass away until all these things be done* (Matt: 24.34). Again, we read in the Apocalypse (22. 10,20): *And he saith to me: Seal not the words of the prophecy of this book. For the time is at hand.* And: *He that giveth testimony of these things saith: Surely I come quickly.*

Vincent also preached the probable imminent advent of Antichrist. In one sermon he says:

"It is of importance to us, because we must enter into conflict; since many arguments show that shortly and swiftly will come the advent of Antichrist and the end of the world."

In Saint Matthew, chapter 24, we read: *For there will arise false christs and false prophets and will show great signs and wonders in so much to deceive, if possible, even the elect.* Therefore, just as Christ was foreshown by type in the Old Testament, so Antichrist will have his types and forerunners; and no one is able to tell when the last type has passed and the final Antichrist has come. Each age has its Christ-followers and Antichrists. Vincent was aware of the Antichrist of his own time, but he could not know that there were more to follow.

This brings us to the reason why the end of the world, although that end is always imminent, has not yet been reached. Speaking of the vision shown to Saint Dominic, when Our Lord appeared to him carrying in His hand three lances with which to end the world, but was stayed by Our Lady who indicated the two founders of the Dominicans and Franciscans, Vincent says:

"By revelation it is manifestly shown that the whole duration of the world rests on a certain conditional prolongation obtained by the Virgin Mary in the hope of the conversion and correction of the world by the aforesaid Orders."

If Saint Vincent's commission was a truly God-given one, then the duration of the world was again prolonged in his lifetime, because the countries through which he preached the approaching Judgment fulfilled the conditions of conversion and correction. As we read in the Book of Jonas, when the prophet was excusing himself to God for disobeying His command to preach forty days before the destruction of Nineveh: *And Jonas prayed to the Lord and said, I beseech Thee, O Lord, is not this what I said when I was yet in my own country? Therefore I went before to flee into Tharsis; for I know that Thou art a gracious and merciful God, patient and of much compassion and easy to forgive evil.*

Ever since the time of the Apostles the world has been warned: *But the end of all is at hand; be prudent therefore and watch in prayers* (I Pet: 4.7). Conversion and penance have brought reprieve after reprieve; but the time will come when the last reprieve has been granted, and the end of all will follow.

Saint Vincent, in specific terms, applied to himself the text of the Apocalypse (14.6): *And I saw another Angel flying through the midst of heaven having the eternal Gospel to preach unto them that sit upon the earth and over every nation and tribe and tongue and people. Saying with a loud voice: Fear the Lord and give him honor because the hour of his judgment is come.* Once at least, Vincent confirmed his right to this title by a miracle.

He was preaching one day in Salamanca on a hill called the Mount of Olives, which happened to form part of the garden of the Dominican priory. Assuring his hearers that the Day of Judgment was near, he proclaimed himself the Messenger of the Judgment spoken of in the Apocalypse. During the sermon a funeral procession had passed, bringing a dead woman to the Church of Saint Paul. Acting under inspiration the master told the bearers who, their business of internment over, were stopping to listen to the sermon, to open the grave and bring the body to the foot of the platform.

Then, speaking in a voice loud enough to be heard above

the murmurs of a crowd indignant that he should take to himself such a title, he said:

"Dead woman, arise and tell these people whether or no I am the Messenger of the Apocalypse sent to preach the advent of the Last Day."     .

The woman rose in her coffin, sat up and answered:

"Yes, Father, you are that Messenger." And immediately the body fell back again rigid and lifeless.

Vincent continued to preach the approach of the Day of Judgment in sermon after sermon, until at last complaints were made to Benedict XIII, who demanded an explanation. In a carefully reasoned letter, Vincent the theologian explained why he considered the end of the world imminent. His explanation must have proved satisfactory to Benedict, for Vincent continued to preach; in fact, according to Père Fages, almost immediately afterwards he wrote the plans of four sermons on the same subject, which are found in the Perusian MSS. following directly on the copy of the letter. The Universal Church, who canonized the saint, by this very fact confirms this letter. In support of his claim to be the messenger of the Judgment Vincent adduces the prodigies which God has worked through him in testimony of the authenticity of his witness.

The whole matter is of such paramount importance as to require most careful study. First there is the messenger himself. Apart from the fact of his being a canonized saint, do the very full details that we possess of his life prove him to be a man who, from his integrity, his knowledge, his realistic outlook and balance of mind, impresses us as one on whom we can absolutely rely? If the witness is satisfactory, is his message equally so? The following chapters give a typical sermon on the approaching end of the world, and his letter to Benedict, the considered statement of one who is proving his right to preach as he is doing. Are these convincing? Have they not an equal bearing on the present time?

Vincent adduces the signs he works in proof of the authenticity of his preaching. Are these miracles, given in the account of his journeys, sufficiently convincing for us to say with all our hearts: Indeed God has set His seal on this man and his work? The third part of this book should be read with the object of making this test.

Then, if we are satisfied with the man, his message and his credentials, since truth is one and indivisible—unity amidst the variety which differences of time and place necessitate—the message which Vincent Ferrer delivered to the peoples of France, Spain and Italy five hundred years ago is also delivered to us now. Are the signs of the approaching end visible to us now as they were then? If so, in God's name, let us beg the saint to show us how, if it be consonant with the Mercy and Justice of God, we may yet win one more reprieve, a reprieve which we know will be conditional only on conversion and correction.

# Chapter XI

## Sermon on the Last Judgment

*This entire chapter consists of a sermon given on the first Sunday in Advent; on the last judgment.* "Our sermon will be on today's gospel, which consists entirely in the doctrine and instruction of Jesus Christ Himself. In this gospel He warns us of the great evils and tribulations which are to come at the end of the world, and tells us of the signs which will precede His coming in judgment. This subject will, I think, be of service to us. Let us begin with the Hail Mary.

" 'There will be signs in the sun and in the moon and in the stars.'

"By study of Holy Scripture and by factual experience we know that when any great and heavy affliction is about to come on the world, often some warning sign is shown in the sky or in the upper air. And this happens by the mercy of God, so that people forewarned of impending tribulation by means of these signs, through prayer and good works, may obtain in the tribunal of mercy a reversal of the sentence passed against them by God the Judge in the heavenly courts; or at least by penance and amendment of life, may prepare themselves against the impending affliction.

102

"So, before the coming of any great mortality, phantom battles are seen in the sky; before famine there are earthquakes; and before a country is laid waste dreadful portents are seen. We are told of the terrible signs shown to the Jews for a length of time before the destruction of Jerusalem under Antiochus. 'And it came to pass that through the whole city of Jerusalem for the space of forty days there were seen horsemen running in the air, in gilded raiment armed with spears like bands of soldiers. And horses set in ranks, running one against another, with the shakings of shields, and a multitude of men in helmets, with drawn swords, and casting of darts, and glittering of golden armor, and of harness of all sorts' (II Mach: 5. 2,3). After this, Antiochus plundered the temple and slew the Jews. Therefore we read in Exodus (7.3): 'And shall multiply signs and wonders in the land of Egypt.'

"Now among all afflictions, three of the greatest and most terrible are shortly to come upon mankind: first, the affliction of Antichrist, a man but a diabolical one; second, the destruction by fire of the terrestrial world; third, the universal Judgment. And with these tribulations the world will come to an end. Therefore, according to the rule of divine Providence, as set out above, before these three, there will be warning signs in the heavens, in the sun and in the moon and in the stars, as is set out in our text.

"The first affliction to come on the world in a short space of time is the advent of Antichrist, a diabolical man, who will bring distress on the whole world as is implied in today's gospel where it is said: 'And upon the earth distress of nations, by reason of the confusion of the roaring of the sea and of the waves.'

"In my text there are four clauses in which we are warned of the four ways in which Antichrist will deceive

103

Christians. The first clause is this: 'There will be signs in the sun.' You must know that in Holy Scripture Christ is called the Sun, and this is because, by the evidence of your own eyes, the sun is among the most beautiful of the creatures made by God. Taking the word etymologically, we have: S-O-L (*Super omnia lucens*), 'Shining above all things.' In the same way, Christ is more beautiful than all the saints, and shines above them all in the brightness of glory, not only inasmuch as He is God, but also as man. And as all the stars receive their light from the sun, who depends on nothing for its own brightness, so all the saints receive from Christ the brightness of glory, strength, sanctity, wisdom, understanding and influence. This is the reason why Christ is called the Sun, and under the same name of 'Sun' God the Father sent Him into the world, saying: 'But unto you who fear my name the Sun of Justice shall arise' (Malach: 4.2). This is not said of the natural sun. For the Church says in praise of the 'Virgin Mary': 'For thou art happy, holy Virgin Mary, and most worthy of all praise, for out of thee has arisen the Sun of Justice, Christ, Our Lord.'

"The first clause tells us that there will be signs in the sun in the time of Antichrist; that is, there will be signs in Christ, and the precise sign is given by Saint Matthew saying: 'The sun will not give its light.' Such darkening does not happen with regard to the sun itself, for it is not in the nature of the sun to be darkened in itself. But by the interposition of clouds and vapor between the sun and the earth the sun appears to be obscured. In the same way, in the time of Antichrist, the Sun of Justice will be obscured by the interposition of temporal goods and the wealth which Antichrist will bestow on the world, inasmuch as the brightness of faith in Jesus Christ and the glow of good lives will no longer shine among Christians. For, lest they should lose their dominion, temporal rulers, kings and princes will range themselves on the side of Antichrist. In like manner, prelates for fear of losing their dignities, and religious and priests to gain honors and riches, will forsake the Faith of Christ and adhere to Antichrist. Now he will be a veritable man, but so proud that, not only will he desire to have universal dominion in the whole world, but will even demand to be called a god, and will insist on receiving divine worship. This we may gather from the second Epistle of Saint Paul to the Thessalonians (2.3): 'For unless there come a revolt first, and the man of sin is revealed, the son of perdition, who opposeth and is lifted up above all that is called God or that is worshipped, so that he sitteth in the temple of God, shewing himself as if he were a god.'

"This will come about because Antichrist by the ministry of demons will possess all the gold and silver of the earth and seas, and pearls and all the precious stones that are in the world. As we read in Daniel (11.43): 'And he shall have power over the treasures of gold and silver and all the precious stones of Egypt.' With this wealth he will gather together in arms all the nations of the world, to fight against those who oppose him. As we read in the Apocalypse (20.7): 'He shall go forth and seduce the nations which are over the four quarters of the earth, Gog, and Magog; and shall gather there together to battle the number of whom is as the sand of the sea.'

"Observe that he will seduce the peoples, that is, with gold and silver and honors; Gog which signifies 'hidden,' and Magog which signifies 'that which is disclosed,' because both hidden and open evil are on his side. Then temporal lords and ecclesiastical prelates, for fear of losing power or position, will be on his side, since there will exist neither king nor prelate unless he wills it. For the same reason,

105

religious, priests and laity will also uphold him. There will indeed be signs in the Sun of Justice, for then it will be obscured in the hearts of Christians, since from those hearts it will not give forth the light of Faith; all preaching of a better life will cease, owing to the interposition of the vapor and clouds of temporal goods. As we are told in Daniel (11.39): 'He will multiply glory and will give them power in many things and divide up the earth at his pleasure.'

"I am asked why God permits this error among Christians, since He is God and the strongest cannot stand against Him? I answer by a dictum of theology taken from the Book of Wisdom (11.17): 'By what things a man sinneth, by the same also is he tormented.' How do the peoples of the world sin against God today? They sin in order to gain honors, dignities and riches. Therefore, by honors, riches and dignities, God permits that Antichrist shall deceive them. If therefore you do not wish to be deceived, now with all your hearts contemn and despise all earthly goods, and long for those of heaven, considering that the goods of this world are transitory and empty, while heavenly and celestial goods are eternal. In this way you will be strong. Saint John gives this counsel: 'Love not the world nor the things that are in the world. If any man loves the world the charity of the Father is not in him. And the world passeth and the concupiscence thereof' (I John: 2. 15-17).

"The second clause says that there will be signs in the moon. You must understand that in the Holy Scriptures the moon signifies our holy Mother the Universal Church, which implies the world-wide union of Christians; for when men speak of the Church, they do not speak of the material building, or the stone and the walls which compose it, but of that gathering of the faithful under one Head, which is the Church in reality.

106

"The Church is signified by the moon and its five phases: first there is the new moon, then the waxing moon, next the full moon, to be followed by the waning moon, and lastly the old moon.

"The Church passes through these phases. The new moon signifies the Church of Christ in His own time; and as the new moon when first seen is like a bow-shaped thread with two horns following the sun, so the Church in the time of Christ had at first only two horns: Andrew and Peter who followed Christ. The waxing moon typifies the twelve Apostles, then the seventy-two disciples, then the three thousand converted by Peter on the day of Pentecost and so on. The full moon typifies the acceptance of the Gospel of Christ in every part of the world, in every kingdom and province. David says (Ps: 18.5): 'In the whole world their sound is gone forth, and their words to the ends of the earth.'

"The waning moon typifies the inability of men to preserve what the Apostles had acquired. In the first place, the Church was lessened by the loss of the whole of India, by means of him they called John the Presbyter; the second, Assyria by means of one of their tyrants; the third, Africa by means of Mahomet; the fourth, the Greeks under their Emperor Constantine; the fifth, the Armenians with their king; the sixth, the Georgians with a certain pseudo-prophet; the seventh, the bad example of the Christians led by a certain heresiarch*; the eighth, the Italians with Bartholomew of Bari; the ninth, the French with Peter of Candia.

"The old moon, because the horns are reversed, typifies that the Church is no longer in the state in which Christ founded it. Christ founded the Church in great lowliness and poverty; now all this is turned round to pride, pomp

---

* Probably the Waldenses whom Vincent evangelized in the Alpine countries. We do not know the name of the individual heresiarch.

and vanity, as may be easily seen in every rank of the Church. Mercy and liberality are changed into simony, usury and rapine; chastity becomes licentiousness, uncleanness and corruption; the brightness of virtue is changed into envy and malignity; temperance has become gluttony and voracity; patience has given place to anger, war and divisions among the peoples; diligence is superseded by negligence. Nothing is now left to make matters worse but an eclipse which is caused by the interposition of the earth between the sun and moon such as only occurs at full moon. As Isaias says in 59.2: 'Your sins have put a division between us.' In the time of Antichrist, the Church, typified by the moon, will be eclipsed; because then she will not give her light, since Christians will no longer work miracles by reason of their sanctity; but Antichrist and his followers will work miracles, not true miracles, but false ones having the appearance of true miracles, in order that they may deceive the people. As Saint John says in the Apocalypse (13.13): 'And he did great signs, so that he made also fire to come down from heaven unto the earth in the sight of men,' that is, balls of fire, such as it is within the power of the devil to send down, if God should permit this and does not prevent him; as we read in Job (1.16): 'And while he was yet speaking—another came and said: A fire of God fell from heaven and striking the sheep and the servants hath consumed them.' O! The wonder of the people, this will be the downfall of many.

"You must know that Antichrist will perform other prodigies by the power of demons, and these will be true miracles according to the nature of things in themselves, but false in regard to the definition of miracle (i.e. by the power of God). For he will cause both images and babes of a month old to speak. The followers of Antichrist will question these

108

statues or babies, and they will make answer concerning this lord who has come in the latter times, affirming that he is the saviour. The devil will move their lips and form the words they utter when they declare Antichrist to be the true saviour of the world; and in this way he will cause the destruction of many souls.

"And the Church, typified by the moon, will perform no miracles.

"Some say that such phenomena are not real miracles in the sense that raising the dead to life is a real miracle. I can give concrete examples of the dead being apparently raised to life, but such are only phantoms. For instance, in the same way as Christians raise dead people in the Name of Our Lord Jesus Christ, so your dead father or mother may appear to speak to you; but in these latter times Christians will not be able to work similar miracles. Christ has warned us of these false miracles and signs, saying: 'There will arise false christs and false prophets.' That is to say, the sons of Christians who have already made shipwreck of their faith owing to the gifts of Antichrist. As Saint Matthew says (24.24): 'And they will show great signs and wonders in so much to deceive, if possible, even the elect. Behold I have told you beforehand.'

"Suppose someone should ask: Why does Christ permit these works of destruction of Christianity by the devil? I answer according to the rule of Theology: 'By what things a man sinneth, by the same also is he tormented.' Since the people of the world sin against God by having recourse to the works of the devil, such as divination and fortune-telling in their necessities—for instance, in order to find things they have lost, or to obtain health or children, instead of laying their needs before the omnipotent God—therefore God permits them to be deceived by the works of the demons.

109

"If you do not wish to be deceived, then place the whole of your faith and confidence in the name of Jesus Christ, and refuse to acknowledge any miracle unless it is worked in that same name; and so you will be strong against seduction. David says (Ps: 39.5): 'Blessed is the man whose hope is in the name of the Lord; and who hath not regard to vanities and lying follies.' The name of the Lord is Jesus. 'And thou shalt call His name Jesus' (Luke: 2.21). If you should receive any wound or hurt you should sign it devoutly with the Sign of the Cross.

"Antichrist arrogates to himself every other name of Christ, but as many of the saints tell us, he flies from the name of Jesus. Therefore, for that reason, the name of Jesus should receive the greatest respect from all Christians. Moreover, all the names of God, according to Saint Thomas Aquinas, should be honored in a sevenfold manner. Because the name of God is great it is to be feared; because it is holy it should be venerated; because it is sweet it should be savored in meditation; it is strong to save; rich in mercy; efficacious in impetration; and hidden in order to be discovered and known. He says also that the name of the Son of God is also the name of the father in a threefold way: for by it he is honored, invoked and manifested. He also says that in all the names given is also signified the name of Jesus, which is the sign of salvation, and therefore exceedingly to be honored.

"The third clause says that there will be signs in the stars. In the Sacred Scriptures 'star' signifies 'light-giving'; and so it is the appellation of Masters, Doctors, and Licentiates in Theology. This signification is found in Daniel (12.3): 'And they that are learned shall shine as the brightness of the firmament; and they that instruct many to justice, as stars for all eternity.' In these stars, that is learned men, there

will be signs in the time of Antichrist; because, as Christ
says in the Gospel of Saint Matthew (24.29): 'Stars shall
fall from heaven'; and this is the third combat waged by
Antichrist, that of disputation.   Then stars, that is the
learned, shall fall from heaven, that is, from the truth of
the Catholic Faith.  The disputations of Antichrist with the
learned will be based entirely on the text of the Old Testament, and these doctors, so far from being able to answer
him, will not even be able to speak.  Then the stars—the
masters—will fall from heaven, that is from the heights of
the Faith.  For, according to Daniel (11.36): 'And the king
—Antichrist—will do all according to his will and will lift
up and magnify all against God, and against the God of
Gods he will speak great things'; that is, the matter of his
blasphemies will be insoluble so far as men are concerned.

"You may ask again why Christ allows this, that those
who defend the Faith should fail so utterly?  I answer that
Christ allows this for two reasons: first, according to the
rule of theology: 'By what things a man sinneth, by the
same is he tormented'; and this follows from the fact that
masters and teachers no longer care for study of the Bible,
but prefer the study of the poets and other profane works.
The second reason why Christ permits this, is because of the
scandalous and wicked lives and the many sins of learned
men; for in the case of many of them, the greater their
knowledge the greater also is their sin and the worse their
consciences; for they are proud, puffed-up, wine-bibbers and
the rest.  He who can bind a lioness can easily bind a
sheep; if therefore the devil can hold in chains the minds
of the learned by reason of their evil lives, how much easier
is it for him to bind the sheep—that is their tongues—so
that they cannot speak.  The ignorant are in much better
case, for knowledge puffeth up; if therefore you wish to be

strong, embrace the counsel of the Apostle Paul (I Cor: 2.5): 'That your faith might not stand on the wisdom of men but on the power of God.' Reasoning and disputation are good for strengthening the intellect, but not for fortifying belief, since faith must be held from the motive of obedience, because Christ Himself has commanded us, announcing the gospel which the Apostles preached and Holy Mother Church has ordained. Therefore, O Lord, I believe.

"The fourth clause tells us: 'And on earth distress of nations by reason of the confusion of the roaring of the sea and of the waves.' Behold these are the tortures which Antichrist will inflict, and on the earth distress of nations by reason of the confusion of the roaring of the sea and of the waves. That is the preparations for battle, the sanding of the arena before the combat, which will be the work of the lords who are already on the side of Antichrist; because then no one will dare to name Christ nor the Virgin Mary under pain of death; and the waves are those of torments which have never in the past been so dreadful as those which will be inflicted by Antichrist. In Saint Matthew, Christ warns us (24.21): 'For there shall then be great tribulation such as hath not been from the beginning of the world until now, neither shall be. And unless those days had been shortened, no flesh should be saved; but for the sake of the elect those days shall be shortened.' We read in the Apocalypse (17:10): 'And when he shall come he must remain a short time.' The Doctors in general say that Antichrist will reign for three and a half years only; which is the measure of a thousand and two hundred days and ninety days; 'and from the time when the continual sacrifice shall be taken away and the abomination unto desolation shall be set up, there shall be one thousand two hundred and ninety days' (Daniel: 12.11).

112

"If I am asked why Christ permits the Christians to be so terribly persecuted, I answer: 'By what things a man sinneth, by the same also is he tormented.' Because now, at the present time, people are offending God by wars, divisions and false flattery, by feuds and duels, so Christ permits them to be torn in pieces and slain by Antichrist. If therefore, you do not wish to be slain and destroyed, be at peace and concord now with everyone, according to the counsel of the Apostle: 'Have peace with all men; revenge not yourselves, my dearly beloved; but give place to wrath, for it is written: "Revenge is mine, I will repay, saith the Lord" ' (Roman: 12.18).

"The second evil or retribution will be the conflagration of the earthly world which is mentioned in the second part of the gospel of this Sunday: 'Men withering away for fear and expectation of what is to come on the whole world; for the powers of heaven will be moved.'

"After Antichrist has been slain by lightning on Mount Olivet and his death has been made widely known throughout the world, this our earth will exist for forty-five more days; I do not say years, but days. This is clearly to be seen in Daniel (12.11): 'And from the time when the continual sacrifice shall be taken away and the abomination of desolation shall be set up, there shall be one thousand, two hundred and ninety days. Blessed is he that waiteth and cometh unto the one thousand, three hundred and thirty-five days.'

"The Doctors say that these forty-five days will be given by God for the conversion of those who have been seduced by Antichrist, but Antichrist will have left behind him so great riches and pleasure that hardly any of the nations will be converted to the Faith of Christ. For there is no saviour but Christ, and yet they will not be converted.

"Then in the four parts of the earth, east, and west, and

113

north, and south, fire will blaze forth by the divine power, and as it presses forward, the whole world in succession will be set on fire until nothing of the other three elements will remain. Then, when men are made aware of the tumult of the fire and see the lightnings bursting forth from it, they will wither away for fear of the fire, and expectation of eternal damnation. The Apostle Paul, in the epistle to the Hebrews (10.27) says of this: 'But a certain dreadful expectation of the Judgment and the rage of a fire shall consume the adversaries.'

" 'For the powers of heaven shall be moved.' This is said to imply that the fire has no natural cause, as some people erroneously imagine, for they say that for forty years before the consummation of the world it will not rain. This fire, however, comes from the rigor of divine justice and acts through the ministry of angels, as it is shewn in the saying: 'For the powers of heaven shall be moved.' This fire comes down, likewise, for the purification of the other three elements—earth, air and water—which have been infected and corrupted by the sins of men. Concerning this, David says (Ps: 96.3): 'A fire shall go before him and shall burn his enemies round about. His lightnings have shone forth to the world; the earth saw and trembled. The mountains melted like wax at the presence of the Lord; at the presence of the Lord of all the earth.'

"You understand how sinners are the enemies of Christ; but why do they say, 'and shall burn his enemies round about,' when the good as well as the bad will be destroyed by the fire? The good and the friends of God will die in the fire it is true, but they will die without pain or suffering; but the wicked and God's enemies will die in the greatest pain and torment. Therefore, the enemies of God are named.

"Saint Thomas Aquinas speaks beautifully of this when

114

he says that this last fire, inasmuch as it precedes the Judgment, will act as an instrument of God's justice. It will also act like natural fire, inasmuch as, in its natural power, it will burn both wicked and good and reduce every human body to ashes. Inasmuch as it acts as an instrument of God's justice, it will act in different ways with regard to different people. For the wicked will suffer intensely through the action of the fire, but the good in whom nothing is found which must be purged away will feel no pain from the fire, just as the three children felt nothing in the fiery furnace, although the bodies of these others will not be preserved as were those of the three children. And this will come to pass by the divine power, that without pain or suffering their bodies will be resolved into ashes.

"But the good in whom there is some stain to be purged away will feel the pain of this fire, more or less according to the merits of each. But they will be swiftly purged for three reasons. The first reason is that in them little evil is found, for they have been already in great measure purged by the preceding tribulations and persecutions. The second is that the living will voluntarily endure the pain; and suffering willingly endured in this life remits much more quickly than suffering inflicted after death. This is seen in the case of the martyrs, for if, when they came to die, anything worthy of purgation was found, it was cut away by the pruning knife of their sufferings. And the sufferings of the martyrs were short in comparison with the pains of purgatory. The third reason is that the heat of the fire gains in intensity what it loses through the shortness of the time. But in so far as the fire is active after the Judgment its power only extends over the damned, since all the bodies of the just will be impassible.

"This is a serious thought for those who will not do

penance. In that last day, how greatly the temporal lords and prelates of the Church will desire to do penance when they see the fire. But then such repentance will avail them nothing, because they are acting not from charity, but from servile fear. Therefore, do penance now, forgive injuries, make restitution of any ill-gotten goods, live up to and confess your religion; and let priests obtain breviaries. If it were certain that in a short time this town was going to be destroyed by fire, would you not exchange all your immovable goods for something that you could take away with you? So it is with the world, which in a short while is to be destroyed by fire. Therefore place your hearts in heaven, and your lips by speaking with reverence of God, and your works by doing good. This is Christ's counsel, saying: 'Lay not up to yourselves treasures on earth where the rust and moth devour and thieves break in and steal.' Notice the word 'rust,' which is Antichrist, and 'moth,' which is fire, for these will devour all.

"The third evil will be the tribulation of the universal Judgment which is mentioned in the third part of this gospel. 'Then shall they see the Son of Man coming in the clouds with great power and majesty.' After the destruction of the world by fire, Christ the Lord Judge, with the Virgin Mary and all the saints, will come to the Judgment seated on a throne in the air. And the Archangel Michael will cry with a loud voice, saying: 'Arise, ye dead, and come to judgment.'

"Then suddenly, by the divine power, all the dead, both good and wicked, will arise, children will rise with grown people and all will be gathered to the Judgment. Even those who died in their mother's womb will be there, as Saint Thomas teaches, to accuse those through whose fault they died without Baptism. And the age at which all will rise will be thirty years.

116

"Christ Himself says concerning the General Judgment: 'When the Son of Man shall come in His majesty, and all the angels with Him, then shall He sit upon the seat of His Majesty. And all the nations shall be gathered together before Him; and He shall separate them one from another as the shepherd separates the sheep from the goats; and He shall set the sheep on His right hand and the goats on His left' (Matt: 25. 31-33). And the creed of Saint Athanasius: 'At Whose coming all men must rise with their own bodies; and it will be rendered to every man according to his own deeds; those who have performed good works will go into eternal life, and those who have done evil into eternal fire.'

"The sheep are the good and the goats are the wicked. Christ will say to the sheep on His right hand: 'Come, ye blessed of My Father, possess ye the Kingdom prepared for you from the foundation of the world.' To the goats on His left He will say: 'Depart from Me, ye cursed, into everlasting fire which was prepared for the devil and his angels.'

"The wicked will go into eternal punishment, the just into eternal life. But for the rest, no one will dwell in this world, because those things which are transitory and finite have passed away in their finite condition; movement has passed away.

"Therefore, the Church in the person of every Christian makes petition in the Office for the Dead:

" 'Deliver me, O Lord, from everlasting death, in that tremendous day when the heavens and the earth are moved, when Thou shalt come to judge the world by fire.' "

117

# Chapter XII

## Letter to Benedict XIII Concerning
## the End of the World

*This entire chapter consists of a letter to Benedict XIII; taken from the Appendix to Pere Fages'* Histoire de Saint Vincent Ferrier.

"To our most holy Lord, Benedict XIII, Pope, Brother Vincent Ferrer, Preacher, a useless servant in regard to both preaching and actions, places himself at the feet of His Holiness.

"The Apostle Paul, after fulfilling the mission entrusted to him in preaching the gospel, constrained by revelation, went up to Jerusalem to confer with Peter and the rest. As he himself tells us in the Epistle to the Galatians (Ch. 2): 'Then after fourteen years, I went up again to Jerusalem with Barnabas, taking Titus also with me. And I went up according to revelation and communicated to them the gospel which I preach among the Gentiles; but apart from them who seemed to be something, lest perhaps I should run or had run in vain.' The Apostles also returned from their God-given mission of preaching, in which they had diligently exercised themselves, and 'coming together unto Jesus, related to Him all the things they had done and taught,' as we read in the sixth chapter of the gospel according to Saint Mark. Therefore, in this present letter, I am ex-

118

plaining in all sincerity, to Your Holiness, Christ's Vicar on earth, and the successor of Saint Peter, what I have preached for so long throughout the world, especially in regard to the time of Antichrist and the end of the world; and I do this the more willingly because Your Holiness has so affectionately commanded me to do so.

"Concerning these matters I have, in my sermons, been accustomed to draw four conclusions.

"The first of these is that the death of Antichrist and the end of the world will occur at the same time. The shortness of the duration of the world after the death of Antichrist has led me to this conclusion, for nowhere in the whole Bible or in the writings of the Doctors can I find a longer period assigned by God for the repentance of those whom Antichrist has seduced than forty-five days after his death.

"We read in the Prophecy of Daniel (Ch. 12): 'And from the time when the continual sacrifice shall be taken away and the abomination of desolation shall be set up, there shall be a thousand two hundred and ninety days. Blessed is he that waiteth and cometh unto one thousand three hundred and thirty-five days.' Now, according to the gloss and the commentaries of the Doctors, the first number, to wit, one thousand two hundred and ninety days, equivalent to three and a half years, is the period during which Antichrist reigns as king. Now forty-five is the number which must be added to this to make one thousand three hundred and thirty-five days, and so this number—forty-five —is understood by the Doctors to refer to the duration of the world after the death of Antichrist.

"Some people, certainly, are dubious about this, and for two reasons. In the first place they raise the question as to whether the number forty-five refers to solar days or days of a year's duration, since in some passages of Scripture a

119

day is meant to signify a year. But I can see no reason for this being the case in the instance under consideration, since both numbers occur in the same connection, and it is hardly likely that one should stand for annual and the other for solar days. For the Scripture text (Ezechiel Ch. 38) manifestly implies that after the death of Antichrist—elsewhere called Gog—there will not be a year before the end.

"Other people are doubtful as to whether the duration of the world after the death of Antichrist be not longer than forty-five days since the Scripture does not expressly deny this. But as the Bible does not mention any determinate time other than forty-five days, it seems unreasonable to suppose that there should be more than forty-five days after the death of Antichrist. If people argue that in so short a time his death could not be published throughout the world in order that the nations might be converted and do penance, some answer that this period of forty-five days will not begin until after the death of Antichrist has been published. Others argue that God, who has ordained that number of days to enable people to repent, will suddenly, either by means of angels or through some terrible portent, make known to the whole world the death of Antichrist.

"The second conclusion I draw is that until Antichrist is actually born, the time of his birth will be hidden from mankind. This conclusion is supported by two texts of holy Scripture: the first in the gospel of Saint Matthew (Ch. 24), where His disciples ask Christ: 'Tell us when these things shall come to pass, and what will be the sign of Thy coming and of the end of the world?' Later in the same chapter Christ answers: 'The day and the hour no man knoweth, nor the angels.' The second text is in the Acts (Ch. I), where the disciples ask the same thing and say: 'Lord, wilt Thou at this time restore the Kingdom of Israel?' And Christ answers: 'It is not for you to know the times nor the moments.' These words must be carefully weighed: 'It is not for you to know the times nor the moments.' It is as if one were to say to the Spanish army and its allies: 'It is not your concern to know the time nor the day when there will be war in Tartary or Armenia, since you have no interests in these places which would make such knowledge pertinent.' But on the contrary, it is most vital for the Tartars and Armenians, themselves, even the peasants, to know the time of such a war so that they may be forewarned.

"So, even though there were the most illuminating revelations of the divine Wisdom concerning these matters, it was not necessary for the Apostles and Doctors of the first ages of the Church to know the time of the coming of Antichrist and the end of the world; but after his birth it is expedient for men, even though they be sinners, or so ignorant as to know nothing of the Apostles and Doctors, to know of this birth, so that they may be forewarned and prepared. This is in accordance with the wisdom, mercy and knowledge of God, who from the beginning of the world was accustomed to send messengers to warn men of any great tribulation about to come to pass. Noah was warned before the deluge, Moses before the liberation of Israel, Amos before the destruction of Egypt, and so on. The Saints, Dominic and Francis, and their respective Orders are warned before the coming of Antichrist and the end of the world, since of both of them the liturgy says, that they are supposed to precede the destruction of the world.

"The truth of this conclusion demonstrates the falsity of two opinions. One is the dictum that the same length of time ought to pass after the Incarnation until the end of the world, as elapsed from the creation to the Incarnation. Exponents of this opinion base it on the words of Habacuc

(Ch. 3): 'O Lord, Thy work is in the midst of the years, bring it to life. In the midst of the years Thou shalt make it known; when Thou art angry Thou wilt remember mercy.'

"But this is not in accordance with the gospel texts just quoted, for, since the Doctors agree that the length of time from the creation to the Incarnation was known to the prophets, the Apostles and the Church of God, if it is true that the Incarnation is midway between the beginning and the end, it follows that the time of the end of the world will also be known. This verse of Habacuc should be understood, not of the middle years of the world, but of any human life which, according to Ps. 89, commonly lasts for seventy years.

"And so the middle years of a man's life will be about the age of thirty-three, the age at which Christ suffered. For Our Lord did not will to die as a little one by the hand of Herod, neither did He intend to die in old age, but in the midst of His life; that is at the time of the greatest virility. And so, in this way, in the midst of the years, God gave life to His work by the death of His Son and made known the work of His mercy, since before that time He was angry with the human race. In this sense, Isaias, speaking in the person of Christ, says: 'I have said in the midst of my days I will go down into hell.' For Christ, dying in the flower of His manhood, straightway descended into hell (limbo) for the liberation of the just.

"Or if the words of Habacuc are taken to mean the middle years of the world's existence, the term does not here imply an equality between the preceding and subsequent times, but should be understood as the middle of interposition. For although the destruction of human life took place in the beginning of time, yet its reparation should not be

122

withheld until the end of time, but should take place between these two terminals. The blessed Gregory uses this
mode of speaking when he says that Christ rose from the
dead in the middle of the night, since He rose at dawn
which stands between the beginning of night and its end,
that is by interposition not equality.

"Others say that there will be as many years from the
birth of Christ to the end of the world as there are verses
in the psalter. Thus the exponents of this theory suggest
that the first verse of the first psalm *Beatus vir* is a prophecy of the first year after the Nativity, and the second verse
a prophecy of the second one and so on. This opinion, however, must be rejected like the first, as it has no foundation
except in presumption of heart.

"The third conclusion to which I have come is that the
coming of Antichrist and the end of the world are near. We
may draw this conclusion from the revelation made to the
two Saints, Dominic and Francis, and also to many others
when these two patriarchs came before the Sovereign Pontiff to ask for the confirmation of their Orders. There is,
for instance, the incident of the three lances with which
Christ threatened the destruction of the world, as we read
at greater length in the histories of these two saints.* If the

---

* An extract from Saint Vincent's sermon on the Feast of Saint
Dominic, which gives this incident in detail is not without interest. One
night, when the Blessed Dominic was praying in a certain church, while
the Blessed Francis was in another, Christ was shown to them with three
lances intending to destroy the world. Whilst, however, these saints were
saying within themselves: "Oh, is there no saint in heaven who will
appease Christ's anger?" suddenly the Virgin Mary appeared, just as a
woman might do to snatch her child from the jaws of a wolf. "Oh
Son," she said, "are you now carrying lances in those hands which are
accustomed to carry nails for the salvation of the world?" In the hearing of Dominic and Francis, Christ answered: "Mother mine, what
more is there that I ought to do, since I have poured so many graces
on the world? I have sent patriarchs and prophets, and they slew them;
finally I came myself to redeem the world. Now I will no longer spare
it." These three lances are the three great tribulations shortly to come

words of Christ and of His Blessed Mother are well studied, these three lances for the destruction of the world are: first, the persecution of Antichrist, second, the destruction of the world by fire, third, the Last Judgment.

"The same conclusion is reached with more exactitude by studying the revelation made to Saint John in the Apocalypse (Ch. 20): 'I saw an angel coming down from heaven, having the key of the abyss and a great chain in his hand, and he seized the dragon, the old serpent, who is the devil and Satan, and bound him for a thousand years, and after that he must be loosed for a short time.' The ordinary gloss explains this shutting up and binding chiefly by the death of Christ on the Cross and His descent into hell, and reckons a thousand years to mean a multitude of years, taking the determinate to signify the indeterminate, that is that a thousand years is looked upon as signifying the whole time from the death of Christ to the coming of Antichrist, when Satan will be loosed for the temptation and seduction of mankind. Nevertheless, this binding of Satan may be very properly understood of his binding, lest he should have tempted or seduced the nations by means of the persecution of the faithful under the Roman emperors. This binding occurred in the time of the blessed Pope Sylvester when Constantine became a Christian and gave the Church her patrimony. For, from that time until the founding of the Orders of Franciscans and Dominicans is a thousand years, and after

---

on the world, namely the coming of Antichrist, the burning up of the world, and the Judgment by Jesus Christ. Now this world is the traitor son of God, acting contrary to His commands, and driving our God his Father from the world as far as he is able. The general of the heavenly armies, Christ, will kill them with the three lances mentioned before. For, in the time of Dominic the world was on the point of being destroyed by Christ, when the Virgin Mary placed Dominic there, obtaining one reprieve. Think how the whole world is involved in this one reprieve, which is not of certain duration but given conditionally, that is, on conversion. If it is converted, then all is well; if not it will not be spared again.

that Satan must be loosed. According to this theory, the Angel descending to bind Satan is held to be Pope Sylvester, or rather Christ acting through him.

"There are several opinions which run contrary to this conclusion. One affirms that there will be a drought of forty years duration before the end of the world. This is untenable because in that case the burning of the world would come about as a natural consequence of the exceeding dryness. For, as the deluge did not occur in the ordinary course of events, but through a divine judgment, so also this deluge of fire will be a direct outcome of the divine power; for, according to the Doctors, it will find men living in great prosperity and the world in a state of tranquility, and, according to Saint Jerome, the fire will burn all matter, even water and the sea.

"Others affirm that Elias and Enoch will come before the advent of Antichrist, in order to preach and to warn men against his deceptions. This is false, as may be seen from the Apocalypse (Ch. 11), where it is said of the followers of Antichrist: 'And the holy city they shall tread under foot two and forty months. And I will give unto my two witnesses, and they shall prophesy a thousand two hundred and sixty days in sackcloth.' Now, Elias and Enoch, properly speaking, will not come before the advent of Antichrist, but at the same time, as it is evident both from the text and the gloss that he had already begun to reign.

"Others affirm that the gospel signs ought to precede the coming of Antichrist. According to Saint Luke: 'There shall be signs in the sun and in the moon,' etc. These signs, however, properly speaking, will occur after the death of Antichrist and immediately before the judgment.

"Another objection is that Jerusalem and the Holy Land will be conquered by the Christians before the coming of

Antichrist. Many texts from the Prophet Ezechiel (Ch. 32), and the acts of the Martyr Methodius, seem at first sight to imply that, at the advent of Antichrist, the Holy Land will be in the hands of Christians. But this conquest has already been partially realized by Christian princes, notably by Godfrey de Bouillon; nor does it appear that the numbers and disposition of Christians are such as to enable them to carry the conquest to its conclusion. In fact, the text of Saint Luke (Ch. 21) seems to contradict this: 'Jerusalem shall be trodden under foot by the peoples, until the times of the nations shall be fulfilled.' The words of Ezechiel and Methodius should be understood more in the light of an allegory of the Church Militant and its numbers than of the Holy Land and its provinces.

"Again we are told that all nations will be brought to the one Catholic Faith before the coming of Antichrist. This does not seem to be true, for this conversion will rather take place after the death of Antichrist when, seeing themselves to have been deceived by his falsehoods, men will return to the unity of the Faith. See Ezechiel (Ch. 39): 'I have given thee to the wild beasts, to the birds, and to every fowl and to the beasts of the air to be devoured,' speaking of the death of Antichrist—Gog—'and I will set my glory among all nations; and they shall see my judgment, that I have executed and my hand that I have laid upon them.'

"Another opinion affirms that the gospel of Christ must be preached throughout the world before the coming of Antichrist, according to the text of Saint Matthew (Ch. 24). 'And this gospel of the kingdom shall be preached in the whole world, for a testimony to the nations; and then shall the consummation come.' This text is subject to diverse methods of exposition according to the manifold general preaching of the gospel throughout the world. First it was preached by the Apostles to every creature according to the precept of Christ in the last chapter of Saint Mark. This precept was fulfilled in the time of the Apostles as is shown in the Epistle to the Colossians (Ch. 1): 'In the word of truth, the gospel which has come to you, as also it is in the whole world and bringeth forth fruit and groweth.' And towards the end of the same chapter: 'The gospel which you have heard which is preached to all creation which is under heaven.' And in Romans (Ch. 10): 'Their sound is gone forth unto all the earth.' Then came the consummation of the Jewish people and the destruction of Jerusalem under Titus and Vespasian. In the second place the gospel has been preached and is still being preached daily by the Dominicans and Franciscans. And after this, straightway will come the consummation and destruction of the world by Antichrist and his followers. The third preaching of the gospel throughout the world will take place after the death of Antichrist by certain faithful ones of each nation, who will have been wonderfully preserved by God for the conversion of the rest; and then will come the last consummation of the world.

"The fourth conclusion I have drawn is that the time of Antichrist and the end of the world will take place in a short space of time, a mercifully short space of time and exceedingly quickly. This conclusion, although in substance it is found in the first homily of Saint Gregory, nevertheless, strictly and properly speaking, I prove it in many different ways.

"First, from the revelations made to Saints Dominic and Francis, which I have spoken of previously. By this revelation it is made manifest *that the whole duration of the world rests on a certain conditional prolongation obtained by the Virgin Mary in the hope of the correction and con-*

127

*version of the world by the aforesaid Orders.* For Christ said to the Blessed Virgin: 'Unless the world is corrected and converted by means of these Orders I will no longer spare it.' Since, therefore, the conversion and correction of the world has not followed but rather the reverse, for greater crimes and wickedness abound, and, it must be regretfully admitted, these Religious Orders themselves, who have been given for the conversion and correction of the world, are in reality so moribund and relaxed that little religious observance is kept in them, the observant man must admit that this conclusion is amply proved.

"In the second place the same conclusion is drawn from a certain other revelation (a most certain one to my mind), made just over fifteen years ago to a religious of the Dominican Order. This religious was very ill indeed and was praying lovingly to God for his recovery so that he might again preach the word of God as he had been wont to do with great fervor and ardor. At last, while he was at prayer, these two saints appeared to him as in a dream, at the feet of Christ making great supplication. At length, after they had prayed thus for a long while, Christ rose and, with one on either side, came down to this same religious lying on his bed. Then Christ, touching him caressingly with the finger of His most holy hand, gave him a most definite interior comprehension that, in imitation of these saints, he must go through the world preaching as the Apostles had done, and that He, Christ, would mercifully await this preaching for the conversion and correction of mankind, before the coming of Antichrist. At once, at the touch of Christ's fingers, the aforesaid religious rose up entirely cured of his sickness.

"As he diligently followed the apostolic mission divinely committed to him, Providence, in testimony of the truth, gave this religious, not only numerous signs as he had given

Moses, but also the authority of the divine Scriptures as he had given John the Baptist since, because of the difficulty of this mission and the slight weight of his own unaided testimony, he was greatly in need of help. Hence, of the three divine messengers sent to men by divine Providence under the name of angels, many persons believe him to be the first, of whom John has written: 'And I saw another angel flying through the midst of heaven having the eternal gospel to preach to them that sit upon the earth and over every nation and tongue and tribe and people, saying with a loud voice: "Fear the Lord and give Him honor, because the hour of His judgment is come. And adore ye Him that made heaven and earth, the sea and the fountain and the waters. Let him who is able understand." '

"Since then the aforesaid religious has been travelling for thirteen years over the world, and is still journeying, preaching every day and in many labors, and though he is now an old man, more than sixty years old, he still holds this conclusion as most certain. . . .

"The same conclusion is also shewn me by another revelation which I heard from a certain holy and devout man —as I consider him. When I was preaching in the province of Lombardy for the first time eleven years ago, there came to me from Tuscany a man sent, as he said, by certain most holy hermits of great austerity of life, to tell me that a divine revelation had been made to several of these men that the birth of Antichrist had already occurred, and must be announced to the world so that the faithful might prepare themselves for so dreadful a combat, and so they had sent the aforesaid hermit to me that I might tell the world. If then, as appears from these revelations, it is true that Antichrist had already completed nine years of his accursed life, then it follows that my conclusion is also true.

129

"Another clear revelation which I heard while in Piedmont, told me by a Venetian merchant on whose word I can rely, confirms this conclusion. He was beyond the seas in a certain convent of the Friars Minor, and was attending Vespers on a certain feast day. At the end of Vespers, two little novices, according to their custom, singing the 'Benedicamus Domino,' were visibly rapt in ecstasy for a considerable period of time. At length they cried out together: 'Today, at this hour, Antichrist, the destroyer of the world is born.' This struck those present with fear and amazement, and among those who actually heard it was the Venetian who told me of the occurrence. When I questioned him and made enquiries about this event, I found that it happened nine years previously, and so this is further corroboration of what I have already said.

"This same conclusion is further borne out by many other revelations made to many other devout and spiritual persons. For, travelling as I do, through many regions, provinces, kingdoms, cities and towns, many devout and spiritual persons come to me, referring with certitude to the coming of Antichrist and the end of the world, which they have received in many and very diverse revelations, and in all of these there is the greatest concord.

"Innumerable demons, forced to a confession of the truth have said the same thing. In many parts of the world, I have seen many persons possessed by the devil, who were brought to one of the priests of our company for exorcism. When the priest began to exorcise them they spoke openly of the time of Antichrist, in accordance with what has already been said, crying out loudly and terribly so that all the bystanders could hear them, and declaring that they were forced by Christ and against their own will and malice, to reveal to men the truth as given above, so that they might save themselves by true penance. These revelations have the effect of leading to contrition and penance the numerous Christians standing round. But when the demons are questioned, or even conjured to tell the truth of the birth place of Antichrist, they will not reveal it. . . .

"From all that has been said above, I hold the opinion, which I think to be well founded, though not sufficiently proven for me to preach it, that nine years have already elapsed since the birth of Antichrist. But this I do preach with certitude and security, the Lord confirming my word by many signs, that in an exceedingly short time will come the reign of Antichrist and the end of the world.

"Our Lord Jesus Christ, foreknowing that this doctrine will be unacceptable to carnal persons and the lovers of this world, said in the Gospel of Saint Luke (Ch. 17): 'And it came to pass in the days of Noah, so shall it also be in the days of the Son of Man. They did eat and drink and they married wives and were given in marriage, until the day that Noah entered into the ark, and the flood came and destroyed them all.' The same thing happened in the days of Lot; they ate and drank, they bought and sold, they planted and built. On the day that Lot left Sodom it rained fire and brimstone from heaven and all were destroyed. This will happen on the day when the Son of Man shall be revealed. On that day, whoever is on the roof and his vessels in the house must not come down to take them, and he who is in the field must not return to his house. Remember Lot's wife!

"Again in the First Epistle to the Thessalonians (Ch. 5) we read: 'And the times and moments, brethren, you need not that we should write to you; for you yourselves know perfectly that the day of the Lord will come as a thief in the night. For when they shall say peace and security; then

131

shall destruction come upon them, as the pains of her who is with child. And they shall not flee.'

"This, most Holy Father, is what I am preaching concerning the time of Antichrist and the end of the world, subject to the correction and determination of Your Holiness, whom may the Most High preserve.

"July 7th, 1412."

# part 3

# The Letters of Credential

# Chapter XIII

## Vincent's Second Journey

Concerning Master Vincent's stay in Lyons, we have the letter of the Chapter, *Ad Perpetuam rei memoriam.*

"On Saturday, September 6, 1404, Brother Vincent of the Order of Preachers, Master in Theology, who is travelling through the world preaching the Word of God after the example of the Apostles, arrived at Lyons, and after having celebrated Mass in the Convent of the Friars Preachers, preached solemnly in the cloister of the principal church. On the next day, Sunday, the eve of the Nativity of the Blessed Virgin Mary, in the presence of our Lord and Father in Christ, Philip of Thurey, Archbishop of Lyons, he preached in the same manner before a great concourse of people. On the feast itself, in consequence of the crowd who had come to Lyons to hear the celebrated preacher, he preached on the far side of the bridge of the Rhone, in the great meadow of the Church of the Madeleine. It was wonderful to see such a great crowd.

"The following Tuesday, after a wooden chapel draped

in red and blue had been built, he celebrated Mass there with the utmost solemnity, before the whole concourse of people and in the presence of our most reverend Archbishop. After the Mass he preached magnificently. He continued the course of sermons for a fortnight.

"He preached also to the religious in the churches and their convents. One Friday he preached in the choir of the cathedral to the ecclesiastics only; no lay person was admitted to the sermon. On the last day, after his solemn sermon, instead of entering the town, he went to preach at Saint-Synphorien d'Auzon.

"We ought to add that during his stay in Lyons the multitude of sick who came to him daily was so great that it was impossible to count them. At certain hours he visited the sick who could not come to him, laying his hands upon them and reciting very beautiful and devout prayers, and curing them by the imposition of his hands."

Such wonders did not happen in Lyons only; they happened everywhere all the days of Vincent's life.

In 1405, Benedict XIII visited Genoa on his way to Savona, and on coming by galley to the port was received in state by the Governor appointed by the King of France, the Marshal de Boucicaut, for Genoa in those days belonged to France. From that place the pontiff sent word to Vincent of his arrival, telling him to leave Lyons and join the papal court. Accordingly, Vincent repaired to Genoa, to be received, by the express command of the French King, with the same honors as had been shown to Benedict.

But at that moment, state receptions and pageants were of no interest to the Genoese, for the plague had broken out in the city, and deaths were averaging two hundred and fifteen weekly. Benedict's stay in the stricken city was short, and he was soon on his way, continuing his royal progress by sea to Savona, Monaco, Nice and Marseilles. But Vincent stayed behind, to organize processions of a very different kind. He carried the Blessed Sacrament through the streets, praying the while with tears for the poor victims. For a long while the plague continued, for, according to the chronicles, "The Almighty does not always lift such burdens from the shoulders of sinners." But Vincent stayed and by his example put heart into the local clergy until at last the ravages of the sickness ceased.

It was at Genoa, that people first realized the existence of a daily miracle which had been worked continuously for four or five years. Master Vincent had already travelled through northern Italy, southern France, the Alpine States and a great part of Spain. He had found his way into towns and villages right off the beaten track where the folk spoke as many different patois as there were villages. Everywhere he went he was perfectly understood by all. It was at Genoa, a cosmopolitan port where Greeks, Hungarians, Germans and Italians foregathered—a city where every merchant was accompanied by an interpreter—that the pentecostal crowds, listening to Master Vincent's open-air sermons, realized with astonishment that each one was hearing the preacher speaking, not only in his own language, but in his own native idiom.

Once it was realized what was happening it was not long before this remarkable phenomenon was being discussed with enormous interest right through the town. What was happening? How did it all come about? What language was the preacher using, for all were ready to swear that he was using their native tongue? At last a deputation of the lettered men of Genoa put the question to Vincent himself.

"You are all wrong and all right, my friends," said the friar with a smile, "I am speaking Valencian, my mother tongue; for, except for Latin and a little Hebrew, I know no other than Spanish. It is the good God who has rendered this intelligible to you."

This fact was juridically attested at the process of the saint's canonization by more than a hundred witnesses; they say that it was not merely the general sense that they understood, but they could appreciate every turn of expression, just as though they were listening to a most luminous exposition in their native language. Furthermore, distance made no difference to them, for those on the outskirts of the huge crowds could hear as distinctly as those who were close to the pulpit. And—a still greater wonder—the saint understood them and could give a detailed answer to the most subtle question. But, the crowning point of the marvel, the saint knew and answered unspoken questions. Sometimes a question was written down and tossed on to the platform, to be found unopened next day; sometimes it was merely present in the mind of the auditor. On the following day the question would be answered in detail at the very beginning of the sermon. In the transcripts of his sermons there are constant interpolations giving some question not having direct reference to the subject matter of the sermon, and its answer. It is impossible that any man so occupied as Master Vincent should have time to listen to and remember questions put to him by strangers; such must have been shewn to him through his gift of reading hearts.

A letter from Nicholas de Clemangis to a friend, Reginald Fontanini, gives a fascinating contemporary picture of the saint's life at this time. This Nicholas, who enjoyed a great reputation in his own day for wisdom and probity, was a Doctor of the University of Paris, for a time Benedict's secre-

tary, and known among his fellows as a rigid censor of morals.
He writes:

"Here is a man of whom everyone is speaking, marvellously celebrated and an object for everyone's praise—Vincent Ferrer, in habit, profession and ministry the glory of
the Friars Preachers. When the Sovereign Pontiff was at
Genoa, this man also was there for some time, sowing the
seed of the divine Word. He is held, God so disposing it, in
such esteem by all, whatever their age, dignity or condition,
that they believe that in receiving him they are entertaining
an Angel from Heaven.

"There is no one better versed in the Bible than he is, or
who is able to quote it with greater effect. His words are
so living and ardent that they inflame, as a burning torch,
the hearts of the coldest, and soften the hardest and most
obdurate souls, drawing from them tears of contrition. In
order to render himself more intelligible he uses many ad-
mirable metaphors to clarify difficulties, and for the same
purpose makes use at times of dialogue, insofar as the dignity
of the pulpit and the subject allows.

"What more can I say? The eagerness with which everyone listens to him and watches him is such that, not only in
the towns where he stops, but even in the countryside, the
villages and much more distant places where he halts, everyone goes to his sermons, which by reason of the crowds are
most generally given in the open air, in the largest open
space within reach.

"But if this seems a prodigy, the really stupendous thing
is his evident gift of tongues. Here are the facts:

"Born in Valencia, he comes into Italy; hardly has he
arrived when he begins preaching in the Italian language
with such facility, such understanding, such distinction of

139

speech, that one might have sworn he was an Italian. And the Italians avow that they have as clear an understanding of his language as they have when speaking among themselves. Even the tiny girls understand him.

"You may perhaps suggest that, since he is speaking Italian, it is hardly surprising that the Italians understand him. Perhaps. But you must admit that it is astonishing to find that directly on his arrival, he already has a mastery of the language. In any case, it is certainly amazing that he speaks such fluent Italian that not only the natives understand him, but also people who have not even a smattering of the language. A German has told me that he understood every word he said as though he were speaking German. And I who can only understand a little Italian affirm, for my part, that I could understand him as well as I can understand you.

"But the crowning glory of this man is that his life is in such absolute conformity with his preaching. He is not one of those pharisees who, seated majestically in the chair of Moses, preach what they do not practice. To his teaching of our obligations he adds his own example. 'I chastise my body and bring it under subjection, lest after I have preached to others I myself become a castaway.' A perfect observer of poverty, he possesses nothing, and accepts neither money nor gifts, contenting himself with no more than is strictly necessary. If, in any town he visits, there is a priory of his Order, he stays there; and one never finds him walking abroad in the streets and squares. He usually dines with his own brethren, and it is generally known that he never takes supper. If he is in a village where there is no convent, he stays with the rector of the parish, only asking what the gospel allows. 'The workman is worthy of his hire.'

"He will only accept the clothes that people are only too

140

anxious to give him when his own are so old and so ragged
that he is no longer decent in them; in accordance with
Christ's teaching, he will have neither two tunics nor two
cappas.

"This valiant laborer in the field of God celebrates Mass
daily, and to multiply the talents entrusted to him he daily
sows the seed of the Gospel, following the counsel of the
wise man: 'Sow your seed morning and evening.' He
does not remain long in one place, but goes from province
to province, from town to town, a pilgrim of the divine
Word, gaining an infinite number of souls and leading them
in the way of salvation. Oh! If only, in imitation of this
holy man, all those who exercise the office of preaching
would follow the apostolic institution given by Our Lord
to His Apostles and their successors. Alas! Such a manner
of life is no longer to be found among us.

"And, since it has given me great consolation among the
sorrows of this sad time to see this unparalleled light, I am
wishful to make you a sharer in my joy, by passing this
news on to you. Farewell.

"From Nicholas Clemangis to Reginald Fontanini."

As has already been said, besides the gift of tongues, the
voice of the master was miraculously enabled to carry
clearly for long distances; also the words he uttered seemed
fitted to the peculiar needs of each of his hearers. Some of
his companions also shared his gifts, at least as far as concerned the confessional; and it is in this sense that authors
say that he communicated his miraculous powers to others.

Women of those times set great store on their coiffures,
on the enormous erections, towers and the like, into which
the barbers twisted their unfortunate locks. These marvels
of vanity were so huge and so frail that no woman ever

dreamed of spoiling them with a hat or other covering. Genoese contemporary historians reckon it as the saint's greatest miracle that he succeeded in persuading the women to cover their heads in church.

Everyone—so they tell us—left his or her occupation to go and hear Master Vincent: the workmen left their shops; the lawyers forsook the courts of justice; the laborers left the countryside to take care of itself; and the women—if such can be believed—neglected their toilette. In the summer of 1405, he worked such a miracle in Genoa that he entirely wiped out all extravagances in hair-dressing, and brought all his auditors back to the modesty of which Saint Paul speaks. He introduced the fashion of the mantilla among them.

From Genoa he passed right through the Riviera, settling disputes, healing feuds, everywhere meting out justice and everywhere being absolutely obeyed.

After this there is a gap in contemporary accounts, and the next time we hear of the master, in 1406, he is in the north of France and in Flanders. In all probability he went there by sea, for if he had travelled by land, traces of this journey, like all others, would certainly be found. In the north of France, probably at Caen, he met the English King, Henry IV of Lancaster, and from him obtained permission to preach through that portion of France and Flanders which was under his jurisdiction. From the factual basis of this meeting has sprung a legend of Vincent's visiting England, but it is highly improbable that a man so celebrated throughout Europe would have come and gone from England leaving no record of his visit behind him. Instead of crossing the Channel he almost certainly turned and hurried south again.

For the next few months his journeys are very difficult to

trace. He appears to have been in several places almost simultaneously. At Vercelli, for instance, he made peace between the Guelphs and Ghibellines, for strife there had almost assumed the proportions of civil war. To add to the difficulties, the town being on the confines of the two papal obediences, there were even two archbishops.

In the Lent of 1406 we find him again at Genoa, where Benedict was then residing. Again he made a fruitless attempt to persuade the pontiff to resign. Later in the year, he made a pilgrimage to Compostello, where a strange miracle took place.

A young man was brought to him, strong and healthy, but stone blind. Kneeling at the saint's feet, the young man implored him to cure him.

"Go," said Vincent, "to the cathedral at Orviedo and there, kneeling before the crucifix, tell Our Lord that I have sent you, ask for your cure and you will be heard."

The blind man did not hesitate. Making the journey to Orviedo as quickly as he could, he went straight to the cathedral and kneeling before the crucifix, according as he had been told, said, "O Lord, Brother Vincent has sent me to you to be cured." Our Lord immediately ratified His servant's word.

We next hear of Vincent at Corogne on the coast of Provence. A strange legend still persists in the neighborhood. It is said that one day when the friar was preaching before the collegiate church, in the portico of which stood a much venerated image of the Blessed Virgin, he was moved with horror by the sins of the people, and made this prophecy: "The day will come when the fish of the sea will play in this square." Then in a voice audible to all, the statue made answer: "No, not for so long as I am here."

Only one of the kingdoms of Spain still remained under

Moorish dominion, and that was the province of Granada. Her king, Mahomet IX, hearing of the renown of the preacher, sent ships in search of Vincent conveying a most pressing invitation for him to visit Granada. After searching many ports in Spain and north Italy, the captain found the saint, who had just left Corogne, at a tiny port in Provence, lingering there to dream of his heart's desire of crossing the sea to Africa, there to find a martyr's crown.

After receiving Mahomet's invitation the master remained a while undecided, for both Granada and Africa drew him strongly. Providence made the decision for him, by means of an ulcer which broke out on his leg and thus utterly precluded any hope of his fitness for missionary life beyond the seas. Furthermore, he was so lamed in consequence that he was obliged to make use of a little she-ass, henceforth the inseparable companion of his missionary journeys.

So on this humble mount he entered the court of the Alhambra.

The master began missionary work at once, and he had not preached more than three sermons when, struck by the power of his words, eight thousand Moors asked for Baptism. The King himself was wavering, but he was so shaken by a warning that the Muftis would raise a revolt against him if he became a Christian that he was afraid to follow his conviction. Thereupon Vincent left the country for fear that his presence would endanger the lives of his new converts. Eight years later the King died, without the grace he had refused being offered again.

Passing through Spain, and visiting the cities of Cordova and Seville, Vincent came to a town called Ecija, the scene of an extraordinary happening. Among those who came to his sermons was a rich and influential Jewess. She joined the spell-bound crowds it is true, but she only came to mock him, to interrupt the preacher and disturb his auditors. One day these interruptions grew so insulting that at last, unable to make the disturbance she wished, she began to push her way through the crowd towards the entrance of the church. Those near, furious at her behavior wished to force her to remain, but Vincent said, "Let the woman go, but do those who are under the porch move to one side."

The people moved as he directed, and as soon as the Jewess had reached the porch one of the arches fell in, crushing her beneath its mass. Hurriedly, those near dragged off the stones, to find the body crushed to an unrecognizable pulp. Trembling, partly with fear, partly with horror of the ghastly spectacle, they stood glancing alternately at the master in the pulpit and at the remains at their feet, half hoping yet not daring to ask for a miracle.

But Vincent, praying in his heart, cried out, "Woman, in the name of Jesus Christ, return to life."

In memory of the miracle which followed, after having received Baptism, the Jewess established a foundation under which, each year on Palm Sunday, the anniversary of the miracle, there was a solemn procession, followed by a sermon always preached by a Dominican.

Travelling north through Spain, his path literally strewn with miracles, the master at last reached the Basque country. A charming story is told of his preaching at San Sebastian. A shepherd on the mountainside with his flock was very anxious to hear the famous preacher. So, trusting in the goodness of his purpose, he drew a circle on the ground round the sheep and, forbidding them to go outside it until his return, he made his way down to the town.

What was his amazement at the end of the sermon to hear the preacher make the following comparison: "Just

145

like the shepherd over there, who has left his flock to take care of themselves after making a circle round them, and forbidding them to leave it."

Preaching penance as he went, Vincent journeyed through the Basque country. Here he prophesied the destruction of a town on account of its sins; there his presence arrested the course of the plague which never afterwards returned to the neighborhood. In one place he met a man being led out to execution. At the same moment a funeral procession passed. Knowing by inspiration that the condemned man was innocent, Vincent called on the corpse to testify to the fact. The dead man sat up, pronounced the other innocent and fell back again.

At last, summoned by Benedict to attend an Ecumenical Council that the pontiff had convoked, the master broke his journeyings to go to Perpignan.

# Chapter XIV

## *The Apostolate in Spain*

The sphere of Master Vincent's influence was immense; and because he was always himself, always true, he was equally at home in the court of the Antipope, among the magistrates and civic dignitaries of the towns through which he passed, in the monasteries of Religious, or among the motley crowds of burghers and peasants, Christians, Jews and Moors who thronged to hear him preach.

The duty which brought him from Perpignan to Spain, to Catalonia, was a letter of summons from the king Don Martin:

"Master Vincent: We have a great desire to treat with you on certain matters which it would not be wise to commit to writing. That is why we beg you affectionately, if ever you have felt any regard for us, to come and assist us by your counsels. Your coming will give us special pleasure.

"Given at Barcelona under our seal, the 19th of January, 1409."

On receipt of this letter Vincent immediately set out.

The first halt in the journey was at Elna, where he was asked to arbitrate in a matter of some difficulty. In addition to the usual family feuds and quarrels between town and town, the authorities were engaged in a bitter dispute with their own townsfolk. An annual sum of two hundred florins was due to be paid to Benedict XIII; the townspeople insisted that it was the business of the town treasury to disburse this sum, while the magistrates were equally insistent that it ought to be collected by private impost on the people.

The two parties asked Vincent to arbitrate, and after hearing both sides of the case, he decided against the Town Treasurer in favor of the people. His decision was willingly accepted by all and ratified by the king, because "The Venerable Father and Master in Theology, acting as judge and arbiter, has declared the private persons indemnified."

The master then turned his steps in the direction of Gerona. Everywhere he found the country ripe for harvest, and, since he was Legate a Latere Christi before he was the counsellor of kings, he halted at Collioure, Santa Maria de Ulla, and Torricelli to preach, heal the sick and convert sinners. Don Martin, however, understood Vincent and so, instead of being angry at the delay, he sent the Papal Penitentiary, the Dominican, Francisco Pereira, with confidential letters.

The envoy found him at Gerona where Vincent had just preached one of his sermons on the Judgment to nearly twenty thousand persons. This sermon made such an impression on his auditors that an inscription on the stairway leading to the Friars Preachers' church has preserved forever the words which carried the greatest appeal to his hearers. Here are some extracts from this famous sermon on the text: "Then they shall see the Son of Man coming" (Matthew Ch. 24):

"After we have all been slain by fire which will burn the whole world, we shall remain dead for three days. And the third day we shall all arise with our bodies. And this because, according to Saint Jerome, as Christ alone arose on the third day, so we together will arise three days after the end of the world. As Osee says: 'Come and let us return to the Lord; for He hath taken us and He will heal us; He will strike and He will cure us. He will revive us after two days; on the third day He will raise us up and we shall live in His sight' (Ch. 6.1).

From the sermons; on the last judgment.

"But some ignorant person may say: and how can this be that we shall all rise, since many will have been destroyed by wild beasts, or become the food of fish, or have been burnt up and their ashes scattered to the four winds? I answer: that this question comes from great ignorance. I will give you two examples, one in nature and one in art. The grain of wheat before it is reborn must first die, afterwards it is born again and multiplies. The same happens in art. The silversmith must first melt the gold or silver of which he has already made a goblet and afterwards he makes a lovely vase. And so no one should wonder if God the Silversmith can do the same and that we shall rise again as we were before death. The whole world was created from nothing. As we read in Saint John's Gospel: 'Wonder not at this: for the hour cometh, wherein all that are in their graves shall hear the voice of the Son of God. And they that have done good things shall come forth unto the resurrection of life; but they that have done evil, unto the resurrection of judgment.' He uses the expression 'hour' according to the common usage, for, when speaking of a short time we say 'hour'; since his resurrection will be sudden, for it will be made manifest; and they will rise at the voice of the Son of

God, Who according to Saint Jerome will call: 'Rise, ye dead, come to the judgment . . .'

"At the Judgment all must be there for themselves and none by deputy, since each person will receive for each separate work either the punishment of damnation, or the reward of salvation. As we read in the Epistle to the Corinthians: 'For we must all be manifested before the judgment seat of Christ, that every one may receive the proper things of the body, according as he hath done, whether it be good or evil . . .'

"Now we come to two questions. The first is, after all have been gathered together in person where will the Judgment be held? And I say that it will be in the Valley of Jehosaphat; because Christ will wish to judge in the place where He Himself was judged. As we read in the prophet Joel: 'For behold in those days and in that time when I shall bring back the captivity of Juda and Jerusalem: I will gather together all nations and will bring them down to the valley of Jehosaphat and I will plead with them there for my people, and for my inheritance Israel, whom they have scattered among the nations and have parted my land. And they have cast lots upon my people; and the boy they have put in the stews, and the girl they have sold for wine that they might drink.'

"The next question is how will they go beyond the sea to the valley of Jehosaphat: by the sea in ships or walking by land? I answer that it will not be by ship because all has been destroyed by fire; nor by riding, because nothing composite will remain on the earth but only the pure elements. Therefore we shall be lifted and borne by angels, who are more numerous than men. Many will come down from heaven and each angel will take his own charge. Both good and evil people will be carried by their good angels. It is obvious that they will carry the good, but with regard to the wicked Saint Mark says: 'And then he shall send His angels, and gather together His elect from the ends of the earth to the heights of heaven.' And Saint Matthew: 'So it will be at the end of the world, the Son of Man will send His angels, and they shall gather out of His kingdom all scandals and them that work iniquity.'

"Now there comes a little practical point: How shall we be carried? First I will deal with the wicked, thereafter with the good, in order to leave you consoled. When a wicked man sees his angel coming, he fears him as a criminal does his gaoler and wishes he were already below the earth. Then the angel seizes him by the hair, and strikes a good blow on the ground like an angry retainer, saying as he does so: 'Now rebel, traitor, I shall bear you to Christ Who will condemn you body and soul.' Then shall the Jews say: 'O Fools that we are.' Then shall the words of Zacharias the prophet be fulfilled: 'And they shall look on Him Whom they have pierced. And they shall mourn for Him as one mourneth for an only son; and they shall grieve over Him, as the manner is to grieve for the death of the first-born . . .' And the wicked will be standing with down-cast eyes in the sight of the Lord not daring to look up, as we read in the sixteenth Psalm: 'They have cast Me forth and now they have surrounded Me; they have set their eyes bowing down to the earth.'

"Now I am going to speak of the good. Each angel will come to his charge, who will look at the angel with joy. And the angel will say: 'Come, blessed One . . . Come, now I will bear you to Christ Who will save you both body and soul.' And as they bear their charges away the angels will sing three couplets to commemorate the three works of a good life: first, the forsaking of sin; second, the practice

of good works; third, perseverance therein until the end.
"For the first they will sing:

*Happy day, happy time, happy space,*
*In which thou hast forsaken sin.*

"For the second:

*Happy day, happy time, happy space,*
*In which thou hast adhered to Christ.*

"For the third:

*Happy day, happy time, happy space,*
*In which thou hast fulfilled penance.*

As Saint Luke says in his Gospel: 'When these things shall
come to pass lift up your heads for your redemption is at
hand.'

"Concerning the award of merit or punishment. When
each has been brought into the presence of Christ the Judge,
the examination of reward or punishment is made. And as
in every well-ordered hall of justice before a definitive sentence is given, the judicial process is read in the presence of
the one to be judged, so before Christ a minute process is
read. And this process is each individual conscience, known
now only to God and its owner. Then made manifest to all
so that everyone may read . . .

"We are told not to judge before the time, for now we
ought not to judge anything, nor to spread abroad even
what we know to be true. But then before Christ it will be
another matter. Now you should give thanks to God because
He may give you a veil with which to cover your face, so
that in your confusion your sins may not be seen. And this
veil is penitence. It has four corners: contrition for sins, and
a firm purpose of amendment; also the careful confession of

sins, and the performance of the penance given by the priest, which although it is but small, draws us away from damnation. We read of this veil of penitence in the thirty-first psalm: 'Blessed are they whose iniquities are forgiven and whose sins are covered.' In Confession, by the priest's absolution our sins are remitted as Christ Himself teaches: 'Whose sins you shall forgive they are forgiven; whose sins you shall retain they are retained.'

"And so if you desire that your sins shall not cover you with confusion at the Last Judgment, receive this veil, confess them and with great joy you will see the Son of Man, Jesus Christ."

At Gerona the messenger delivered King Martin's letter to Vincent, who studied it carefully, gave his answer, and then with mind at rest continued on his apostolic journeyings.

Before leaving Gerona he treated his auditors to a dramatic little episode such as often served to engrave his teaching on their hearts. A jealous husband was making his wife's life a burden to her. In fact so unbalanced in mind did he become through groundless suspicion, that he actually blazoned it through the town that a poor babe born to his wife some eight months before was not his own child. In her misery and despair the mother came to seek comfort and advice from the famous preacher. Vincent was nothing if not practical.

"Pray," he told her, "come to my next sermon and bring the baby."

The woman did as she was told and made her way to a place not far from the platform. In the midst of a fine period, the master suddenly broke off, stopped short and looked straight at the child.

"Go and kiss your father," he told the little one.

Immediately the child of eight months left its mother's lap to toddle to an unhappy looking man, glowering in an obscure corner, and held out its arms. The baby was irresistible, and with the touch of its soft cheek, it brought peace and joy back to the home.

Master Vincent's route at this time was determined by the feuds and vendettas with which the country was filled. According to a contemporary historian: "Feuds were numberless, and numberless were those who sought the lives of their enemies; but at the voice of Vincent Ferrer all came together and made peace. And thus it was his custom to re-establish concord wherever he went."

Because of his unique mission, and the necessity of adding weight to his words with the people of his time, miracles literally flowered under his feet, as plentiful as the delicate weeds of the roadside and as astonishing in variety. At Berga, for instance, a shower of rain at the conclusion of an open air sermon drove numbers of people to seek shelter in a bakery kept by a Moor. The women of the company, with more zeal than discretion, began to question the man as to why he had not been present at the sermon. This put the baker, a fervent Moslem, in a terrible rage.

"Just you see what use your saint will be to you," he cried, and throwing a lighted brand on to a pile of wood in the middle of the shed, he shut and bolted the door and went away. The terrified crowd immediately began to cry for help to Master Vincent. At once the flames died down, the baker was converted and with him all the Moslems of the district.

Crossing the mountains between Vicq and Granollers was a painful matter to travellers, for the country was barren and the few villages to be found on the route were of the smallest and poorest description. The master had three

thousand followers at the time and when they reached Lo-
cana and made their way to the poor village inn, the land-
lord was aghast.

"Father," he said, "you are bringing an army with you,
how can you imagine that we have provisions for so many?
I have just five loaves and a flagon of wine, and not the
best wine at that."

"Give what you have, nevertheless, and keep on giving,"
answered the master. And the inn-keeper, doing as he was
bid, found that he had ample for the whole company, and
that the wine he was serving was of the best. The man was
terrified, but he kept his head nevertheless, and when the
meal was over, he asked the master to bless his house. Vincent complied, and at the blessing, corn-bin and wine-cellar
were filled anew.

By the time that Vincent neared Barcelona the whole
town was in a ferment, for the news of all these prodigies
which strewed the path of the apostle had gone before him,
and the city authorities, hearing of the welcome accorded
him in other places, were determined not to be outdone by
any. "For," said they, "considering that everywhere they
have been, those who follow Master Vincent have received
the most lavish hospitality, it would shame our city if, after
having come at our request, we did not prepare for him
the finest welcome possible."

From all the neighboring towns people poured in, and
Vincent preached to them in the Royal Square, the square
itself and all the adjacent streets, every window, every roof
being packed with those who were determined to hear him.
The king, writing to one of his captains, tells him: "For
six weeks now, Barcelona has kept one long feast, such as
I have never seen before, nor have I ever witnessed a like
devotion."

155

Miracles, of course, were not lacking. One who had been a cripple for many years had not the patience to wait for the general audience with the sick, but took hold of the wonderworker as he came down from the pulpit in the garden of the Friars Preachers—this garden, by the way, was utterly destroyed in order to make room for the crowds who flocked to hear the apostle. Vincent hesitated for a moment, then, touched by the faith which had brought the sufferer face to face with him, he made a large Sign of the Cross, and the deformity disappeared forever.

After journeying to Manresa and Lerida, Vincent returned to Barcelona. The plague was raging there and he came to give the comfort of his presence. It was here that he taught the terrified people a prayer to be said in time of sickness.

*From a short lit-*
*any composed*
*against the plague.*
"O Lord Jesus, who desirest the salvation of all men, Thou to whom no prayer is offered without hope of Thy mercy, because from Thy adorable mouth this word was uttered: 'Whatsoever you shall ask of the Father in My name He will give it to you'; by the grace of that same name, grant me at the hour of my death the full possession of my faculties, the use of speech, the most lively sorrow for my sins, a true faith and well-founded hope, a perfect charity, so that from the depths of my heart I can tell thee: 'Lord, into Thy hands I commend my spirit,' Thou Who art blessed and glorified for ever. Amen."

Vincent had not been long in the city before the sickness abated, for, to quote a witness: "Hardly had he roused the people to repentance, when straightway the pestilence ceased."

During Vincent's first stay in Genoa, the Florentines had

156

sent an embassy praying him to come and evangelize the city. Vincent had answered: "Why do you look so far afield for a preacher when you have such a perfect model (the Blessed John Dominici) in your very midst? If you will not hear him, it would be vain for the dead themselves to rise from their tombs. Nevertheless, your interests touch me closely, and one day you shall see me among you."

The master was setting out from Barcelona to fulfill his promise when letters from Ferdinand, the Regent of Castile, made him again defer, this time forever, his promised visit. Turning back on his footsteps, he began to evangelize the country bordering on the shores of the Gulf of Lyons.

At Montblanch, a rugged mountain village in Catalonia, his little ass cast a shoe, and the master applied at a wayside smithy to have her fitted with a new one. After the little beast had been shod, the blacksmith held out his hand for payment. When, however, Vincent contented himself with giving the man a blessing, the latter was so furious at receiving nothing more tangible that he began to curse and swear at the top of his voice. Whereupon, Vincent turning to his mount made her a sign, and immediately lifting up her foot, she shook off the shoe which the smith had so churlishly begrudged her.

At Montblanch there was a deaf man whose inability to hear rendered him so irritable as to induce attacks of frenzy, until at last he grew unable to endure the company of his own kind, for in his fits of madness he would throw himself under the feet of the passers-by. Years before he had been expelled from the town and since then he had lived in solitude, subsisting on leaves and roots until he had lost almost all likeness of a man.

One night, as the poor fellow lay asleep, he dreamed of a man clothed in white who touched him on the ears and restored his hearing. On waking next morning he experienced an unwonted sense of peace. Impelled by some inward urge, he knew not what, he made his way to the town where he had not been for many years. He found the streets deserted, for all the folk were gathered in the square outside the church listening to Friar Vincent. Looking round, he saw in one place a crowd of sick waiting for the friar's blessing at the end of his sermon. The deaf man joined himself to their ranks, and when in his turn the wonder-worker stood before him, he told his dream and the reason of his presence. Vincent listened, stretched out his hand and touched him. The man was cured immediately, and in token of gratitude followed the train of the saint for eight months.

In the same town, a young mason was working with his father repairing the principal church, Santa Maria. He was high on the scaffolding one day when his foot slipped and he fell. Onlookers quickly ran for the master who stood looking down at the crushed and battered body of the young mason.

"Oh, Man of God!" murmured the poor fellow, "you cure everyone else. Is it possible that you have no mercy for me?" Vincent stooped, made the Sign of the Cross on his forehead, and said to him:

"Have confidence, my son, and life and strength will be given you; but you and your father must finish your work on the church without payment for the love of the Blessed Virgin Mary who has shewn you this favor."

A paralytic, who for fifteen years had been unable to move hand or foot, was cured by Vincent's invoking the Blessed Virgin. Then at his blessing the man rose and went to his own house unaided.

At this time three letters recalled Vincent to Valencia.

# Chapter XV

## *Continuation of the Spanish Apostolate*

"To the very reverend and perfect Brother Vincent Ferrer of the Order of Friars Preachers, master in theology and beloved as a brother:

"Reverend Master and very dear Friend,

"He alone to Whom all is known realizes the consolation which your answer has given to our souls, and the joy that your friendly words have brought. Your charity desires to return to your birthplace to preach the gospel of Jesus Christ. The announcement of your arrival—and please God it will be soon—has caused universal rejoicing. We are particularly happy in the thought of the good which this Christian family will draw from it, and of the cessation of the misfortunes which are tearing it asunder. The perverse children of the Church are constantly afflicted by evils of all kinds, by wars, and such bitter discords that brother takes up arms against brother, murders follow murders, and honest folk are only permitted to live in as far as the audacity of men who fear neither God nor man allows them.

"Providence alone can give a remedy to such great calam-

159

ities, but we consider your intervention necessary. Moreover, we have need of your counsels and support in order to act efficaciously; for we are moved by the public misery to put an end if possible to all this suffering. We beg of your charity and your well known friendship to begin your apostolate in your mother country, and we beg you by the Mercy of God to put on one side anything which may retard your coming among us and the pacification of this country, in order that it may serve God better. May God keep you in His holy grace. The Magistrates of Valencia, ready to serve you.

"Valencia June 12, 1409."

Difficulties were by no means exaggerated in this letter. Family feuds were at their height, and the only respite enjoyed by the towns occurred when the opposing factions were engaged in pitched battles on the plains outside the city walls. Open broils and secret assassinations were the order of the day, and the paying of one blood debt only laid the foundation of another.

Vincent had begun travelling in the direction of Valencia sometime before receiving the letter just quoted, for post travelled slowly in those days and the friar was always on the move. In fact on Good Friday, 1410, he was preaching at Tortosa, and the throng listening to him was so great that they filled the bridge of boats which at that time spanned the Ebro. While this multitude was awaiting the master who was praying in the church, the bridge collapsed under the strain and broke in two. A terrible cry, which reached the preacher in the church, rose as the masses of people were precipitated into the river. With unhurried steps he came to the porch, and one Sign of the Cross repaired the damage. The people struggling in the water suddenly found themselves back on the shore, and the miracle-worker returned to pray.

160

News of this sort travelled quicker than the post and the tale preceded Vincent to Morella, his next stopping place, where the enthusiastic inhabitants, relic-hunting, tore his cappa into ribbons. Before he left Morella he made the following prophecy:

"I tell all of you who are listening to me, that eight days from now a great clap of thunder will resound. It will echo throughout the kingdom and will bring in its wake many violent deaths and a terrible outpouring of human blood." Pressed to explain himself he said:

"Messengers are coming to bring the news of the death of the king."

On the thirty-first of May in 1410, King Martin had died.

From Morella the master proceeded to Cati, where the folk had been preparing for him by mending all the roads on which he had to travel. They went out in their hundreds to meet him, and all the neighboring cities sent in provisions: fish, fowl, eggs and the rest, which a celebrated cook named Macerot was charged to prepare. In return for this hospitality, when Vincent left the town, he made the Sign of the Cross on a marble pedestal, which took the impression of his fingers as easily as if it had been wax.

"My children," he said, "I have preached penance to you, now go back to your homes. And to show you that this time I expect my admonitions to be obeyed, I have given you a sign that you cannot erase."

In one of his sermons the master explains the abundance of miracles which we find him working everywhere, charming, terrifying, bizarre, wearisome and fantastic perhaps to our materially-minded generation, but fundamentally as necessary a proof of his message now as in his own simpler day. Speaking of the certitude of our Faith Vincent said:

# ANGEL OF THE JUDGMENT

*From the sermons;*
*on the certitude*
*of our Faith.* "He who wishes to prove any law ought to examine two things, first if it has been approved by divine authority, secondly, if it has been observed by human sanctity. In regard to the first, it is certain that God is not a lying witness. 'God is not like lying man.' But how can we tell that God approves the Faith? I answer, in the same way that a man believes the Letters of a king, because the royal seal is impressed on them; otherwise the Letters would have no authority. In the same way the Truths of Faith are signed by miracles which can be worked by none but God. David says: 'Thy testimony is entirely to be credited.' It was otherwise in the Law of Moses, because such miracles —e.g. the rod turned serpent—can be worked even by creatures. We see the like in the Mohammedan sect. But the Truths of Christianity are confirmed by miracles which can only be worked by God, such as giving sight to the blind, hearing to the deaf, raising the dead to life."

As Jesus Christ worked such miracles in testimony of the truth of His teaching, so His apostle Vincent by the power of God worked miracles of like nature, in testimony of the identity of his teaching with that of Christ.

Still making his way towards Valencia, Vincent stopped to preach at Nules. During the sermon delivered according to custom in the open air, one of the overloaded tiers of a stand fell, without, however, doing anyone the smallest harm; the saint meanwhile continuing his sermon. This was not the only time that such harmless accidents occurred. Speaking of this one day, the master said:

*From the sermons;*
*on the occurrence*
*of miracles.* "I will answer a question which has been put to me: Why, before I begin Mass, do I make a Sign of the Cross in the direction of those who listen to me who are standing

162

on any raised platform? For thirteen years I have preached in the open and these things have happened to me. In Savoy on Christmas Day, I was preaching in the castle where the count and countess were staying. Right above the great hall were windows and doors. In the middle of the sermon one of the doors fell on my auditors and did no more harm than if it had been a match. In another town, there was a very high balcony which could only be reached by a mere catwalk; the balcony fell harmlessly on the crowd. At Reus near Tarragona a balcony fell without hurting anyone. At Chinchilla we were delivered from a still greater peril. That is why you must not be astonished when you see me make the Sign of the Cross. No danger can lead to harm if that sign is made."

But Valencia was growing more and more impatient as the letters which followed Vincent on his travels show. At last to clinch the matter the magistrates even fixed the day on which they would expect him. He was to preach on June 24th, the Nativity of Saint John the Baptist, in the church dedicated to that saint.

Eventually, Vincent actually arrived on June 23rd and was lodged in the Abbey of Saint John near the square where he was to preach next morning, for no church could possibly hold the masses of people who were flocking to hear him. His sermons were, as always, sealed with miracles. There was one, however, which he refused to work.

One day a beggar girl, dumb from birth, was brought to him.

"What do you want, my child?" asked Vincent.

"My daily bread, and the gift of speech," answered the dumb girl.

"You shall have your daily bread," rejoined the master,

163

"but as for the gift of speech, you know perfectly well by the bitterness of your thoughts that you would make bad use of it. Go and thank God for what He has done for you, and put out of your mind any idea of asking Him for something which would be bad for you."

The girl bowed her head and went away, to live seven more years a model of patience and piety.

The master remained in Valencia for two months and then continued his journey south along the sea coast. The inhabitants of Teulada not far from Cape Martin, had for many years suffered a double scourge, a yearly visitation of the plague, and incursions of Moorish pirates.

Vincent took a boat out to a rock in mid-sea outside the harbor. On it he made the Sign of the Cross, saying:

"Rest assured that pirates will never pass this rock." On his return the master made his way to a spot outside the village where four crossroads met; from there he blessed the countryside and set up a wayside Cross beyond which the plague never came again.

At Liria there was such a drought that the Town Council was obliged to order the water to be measured out to each person. They begged the help of the Master. Vincent ordered a three-day fast, and he blessed the one well in the town according to a liturgical formula still in use.

After this he promised the people that water should never fail them. At times there might be a diminution, but sufficiency would always remain. This promise has been fulfilled to the present day.

Travelling between Alcoy and Alicante, Vincent and his company had to cross an arid region. The way was long and dusty, all were very thirsty, and after a time the spiritual temperature began to lower in proportion as the material one grew higher. Faces fell, feet dragged and boredom

164

# *Our Lady of Fatima*

Statue by American Sculptor Frederick Shrady. Unveiled at Vatican Gardens on the Feast of Our Lady of Fatima May 13, 1983 by Pope John Paul II. A duplicate statue cast from the same mold unveiled by Most Reverend Howard J. Hubbard, Bishop of Albany at Our Lady of Martyrs Shrine, Auriesville, New York, May 29, 1983.

IMMACULATE
HEART OF MARY
BE MY
SALVATION!

# Prayer to the Immaculate Heart of Mary
## by His Holiness Pope John Paul II

Oh, Immaculate Heart! Help us to conquer the menace of evil, which so easily takes root in the hearts of the people of today, and whose immeasurable effects already weigh down upon our modern world and seem to block the paths towards the future!

*From famine and war, deliver us.*

*From nuclear war, from incalculable self-destruction, from every kind of war, deliver us.*

*From sins against the life of man from its very beginning, deliver us.*

*From hatred and from the demeaning of the dignity of the children of God, deliver us.*

*From every kind of injustice in the life of society, both national and international, deliver us.*

*From readiness to trample on the commandments of God, deliver us.*

*From attempts to stifle in human hearts the very truth of God, deliver us.*

*From sins against the Holy Spirit, deliver us, deliver us.*

Accept, O Mother of Christ, this cry laden with the sufferings of all individual human beings, laden with the sufferings of whole societies.

Let there be revealed, once more, in the history of the world your infinite power of merciful Love. May it put a stop to evil. May it transform consciences. May your Immaculate Heart reveal for all the light of Hope.

*The Holy Father sent up this memorable prayer to Our Lady at the end of the Consecration of the World to the Immaculate Heart of Mary at Fatima, May 13, 1982 to save the modern world from the attacks of evil that threaten to destroy it*

*With Ecclesiastical Approval*
Published for Our Lady of Martyrs Shrine – Auriesville, New York 120

began to reign. The master was watching, quick to understand the trouble. After all, man is not merely spiritual soul but animal body informed by spiritual soul.

"Take courage, my children," he said. "Beyond the hill you will find a suitable place in which to rest."

And indeed, beyond the summit of the hill, they came to a fine looking inn which appeared to be newly built where the food and the service were perfect and where they were able to rest.

There was among the company a young man to whom the daily miracles that he saw made no appeal. After the company had started and had left the inn some distance behind, Vincent asked this man to go back and fetch the skull-cap he had left behind there. Happy to serve his master the other retraced his steps, no difficult matter since it merely meant turning back on the tracks of several hundred persons.

But what was his amazement, on reaching the hill, to find no inn nor anything approaching a dwelling of any sort. It was the same place, the landmarks were all there, but it was a bare stony lonely hill top, peopled only by birds. The young man stared round stupefied, and his stupefaction was by no means lessened when he saw the cap he had been sent for hanging suspended from one of the stunted trees. Then the young man, taking a deep breath, understood, and hurrying back with the cap, begged the master's pardon for his unbelief.

"Good!" said Vincent. "But do not breathe a word of this to anyone."

Nevertheless, it was not long before all the company knew that the inn had been providential in the fullest sense of the word, and that they had been served by angels.

Another skull-cap of Vincent's left behind by him at Alcoy was found very efficacious for the safe delivery of

165

women in danger in child-bed. For three years it was passed from hand to hand until at last someone stole it, for it disappeared and its owner could not trace it. At last one night, during a terrible storm, someone tapped at the door of the owner, and an unknown hand threw the cap in at the door.

# Chapter XVI

## *The Last Part of the Spanish Apostolate*

Another letter, such as he was accustomed to receive, reached Vincent from Orihuela at the end of August, 1410.

"Very Reverend Father in Jesus Christ,

"We have learnt from our neighbors of how in Valencia and elsewhere, by the help of God, you have put an end to innumerable evils, and fostered virtue and good works without measure. That is why, Reverend Father, we are writing to you, for we know that all those who have heard you have returned to the truth and have left crooked paths for the straight way, and we beg you to come here. For this place is full of vice and the grossest forms of superstition, such as belief in divination and the like. So, as we ourselves are anxious to banish so much crime, at the request of many of the townspeople we have sent to you one of our number, Don Jaime Torres, and we beg your charity to receive him favorably, and to accept all that he tells you as coming from us. We shall be most grateful."

Vincent came as he was asked, to be met with honor at the city gate and to give the usual sign-manual of his divine commission by working miracle after miracle as he entered the city. As the chronicler says: "Each step was marked by prodigies, and he was received as an angel of God." An account of his stay as given in a letter from the magistrates of the city has already been given in Chapter X. At Murcia, where he preached on Easter Eve, a strange thing happened. He was preaching in the great square and ten thousand persons were listening absorbed. Suddenly, the approaching gallop of horses was heard accompanied by wild neighing. Soon the people saw a cloud of dust, and in the midst of the cloud they could distinctly see approaching three horses, covered in foam, with fiery eyes, flying manes, and distended nostrils. Forward they thundered until they were not more than twenty paces away from the dense mass of people. There was a moment of almost unendurable terror.

"Make the Sign of the Cross," cried the master, and ten thousand hands were raised at once. The preacher himself blessed the crowd in the direction from which the danger came. At this the three horses stopped dead, and then turning quickly, made off in another direction; and for a long time the thunder of their hoofs could be distinctly heard.

"Those horses," the master told the petrified crowd, "are not animals but supernatural beings, the evil spirits who for too long a time have been masters of this town, thanks to the three chief vices which reign here. They were so furious to see your souls escaping them that they have made one last attempt to injure, or at the least to terrify you. But, as you have just seen, an act of faith is stronger than all the powers of hell." Then after a moment's silence he added: "It is a rare thing, nevertheless, for Satan to return to hell after a visit to earth without having committed some act of mischief. There is a mother among you who was afraid to bring her daughter to hear this sermon. She will have reason to repent her cowardice."

Vincent's words were justified in the event. For, on returning home, the mother in question found that a man had forced his way into the house, and that the girl had lost that virtue which she had not been taught to defend.

When on the point of departure from Murcia, Vincent caught a cold in his throat which left him for some time with recurrent fits of hoarseness. As soon as he was able to speak again, he took this attack of laryngitis for the theme of a sermon; no wonder the folk loved to hear him. Here is the sermon:

" 'He discovered to them the hidden meaning.'

"My friends, I intend to tell you the cause of my hoarseness, for in it I find good material for instruction, which should benefit both Christians and Jews. Let us say the 'Hail Mary.'

"Let me first explain the literal sense of my text, for it recalls one of Our Saviour's great miracles. His disciples were earthly-minded men, unable to understand the mysteries of the Sacred Scriptures and the writings of the prophets; and so His first care after His resurrection was to make clear to them their hidden meaning. Now to open the eye of the intellect is a far greater miracle than to open the eyes of the body.

"It was Easter Sunday. Our Lord appeared to His disciples and signed them on the forehead saying: 'Let your minds be open.' And with the eye of the mind they saw clearly. He had already told them: 'I will give you a word

*From the sermons; on his laryngitis and his ability to speak.*

and wisdom which no one shall be able to resist.' And in the Old Testament: 'Bind up the testimony, seal the law among My disciples. . . . Behold I and My children whom the Lord hath given Me for a sign, and a wonder in Israel from the Lord of Hosts, Who dwelleth in Mount Sion.'

"That is the literal sense of the text; but I wish to apply it to my sore throat and I will give you my reasons. There are three. The first is particular and has reference to myself; the second is general and has reference to all of you; the third is special and has reference to the Jews.

"First with reference to myself. You must know that there is, so to speak, only one virtue, and without this the others are lost in the same way that corn is lost in a sack with a hole in it; and that virtue is humility. That is why we must be lowly, without hypocrisy or vainglory, having our hearts always open before God and desiring nothing but His honor. David and Saul furnish examples of this and there are other authorities to be found both in the Old and the New Testament: 'The greater thou art, the more humble thyself in all things and thou shalt find grace before God,' says Ecclesiasticus. 'God resisteth the proud and giveth His grace to the humble,' says Saint Peter. This is proof that only humility can preserve the creature in the friendship of God. That is why, when God chooses someone for His service, He places obstacles in his path in proportion to his desires, in order that he may be humbled, and vainglory shall not make void his work. Moses, when the Lord made him stammer, is an example of this. 'Lord,' he said, 'what is this? Since Thou hast spoken to Thy servant, I have more impediment and slowness of tongue.'

"Now Moses had to speak to the people, and he was obliged to do it by deputy, that is to say, by his brother Aaron. And he whose lion-heart had enabled him to work

THE LAST PART OF THE SPANISH APOSTOLATE

miracles, now possessed one no bigger than that of an ant, so that he was unable to address the people in his own person. And thus he was humbled and no longer ran the risk of vainglory.

"Saint Paul worked miracles and even raised the dead, but he was unable to rid himself of concupiscence and said: 'Lest the greatness of my revelations should puff me up, a sting of my flesh was given me, an angel of Satan to buffet me.' And so these two great men were bridled with the bit of humility. How much more need have I of this virtue! Poor miserable creature that I am, and so I too must say: 'Lest the number of my sermons should puff me up, this sore throat has been sent to me.'

"The second reason has reference to the souls of those in this city. The salvation of souls is the principal desire of God: 'It is the spirit which quickeneth, the flesh profiteth nothing.' Give me souls and take the rest for yourself. That is why, in view of your salvation, God has sent me this hoarseness. For as you know, I had already left this town with no intention of returning. And I have returned, that I may seek the salvation of souls and that so many good works may follow, such as disciplines, fasts, confessions, in which even children and soldiers have joined. In the twentieth chapter of Saint John's Gospel we read that Christ came from the earthly paradise for the conversion of one man, namely Thomas; therefore, how much more should I, a sinful man, return seven leagues to this city for the conversion of so many. Saint Paul says: 'Wherein I labor even unto bonds as an evil doer. But the Word of God is not bound. Therefore I endure all things for the sake of the elect of God that they also may obtain salvation, which is with Jesus Christ in heavenly glory.' Therefore he discovered to them the hidden sense.

171

"The third reason is special and has reference to the Jews; for God promised Abraham that of his seed the Messias should be born, and He blessed him that he might have that seed; because God had promised Abraham that in his Seed all nations should be blessed. 'All the generations of the earth shall be blessed in thy Seed, because thou hast obeyed My voice.' And so the Jews say: 'We are the seed of Abraham; therefore the benediction belongs to us together with salvation.' But this the Jews do not understand, that all generations are blessed in the seed of Abraham which is in Christ, who took His human body from the seed of Abraham. They are blessed, that is, if they believe and obey; otherwise they will not be blessed in Christ the Seed of Abraham. And therefore, since in the first place the Jews have not yet come to the full knowledge of the Faith, and the resolution of their doubts, God has willed that I should return to this city. And He has given me this impediment of hoarseness; because no other impediment could have held me back, not even a broken leg which would have forced me to go preaching on donkey back. And so, by the Grace of God many have been converted, and I have looked forward to their conversion, for I believe that they already had faith in their hearts, on account of what they had heard of the Trinity, the Incarnation and Passion of Our Lord.

"And so my good people, enter into friendship with these newly baptized Christians that you may instruct them in the Faith. Admit them to the Public Offices as we are told in the Book of Numbers: 'And if thou comest with us, we will give thee what is the best of the riches which the Lord shall deliver to us.'

"And now you have the reasons why I have been hoarse. And so I am able to say: 'He (that is the preacher) opened the sense that they might understand the Scriptures.' *Deo Gratias.*"

Chinchilla carried the remembrance of another topical sermon. The ladies of the town had a most extraordinary style of coiffure. From the piled up crown of hair they hung as many ribbons as they possibly could. These ribbons were about twelve yards long and hung down in all directions. An anecdote in a sermon shamed them out of this ridiculous fashion.

"One day they were taking a man out to hang him. His wife followed in tears. When they had reached the place of execution they found that they had forgotten the rope. 'Wait a while,' said one, 'we have sufficient here following us.' And they hanged him with his wife's ribbons. I do not know whether you have similar head-dresses for a similar purpose."

A delightful little incident occurred when the master was travelling to Ayllon where the court of Castile had its summer residence. When news of his approach reached the city, the civic dignitaries went to meet him on foot, lest their more splendid mounts should shame the little she-ass. At the court he spoke with the greatest frankness, lectured the courtiers, explained their duties to the princes, and finally preached to the people. For the King, Henry III, he traced a magnificent plan of government.

At Zamora, an occurrence took place of such an extraordinary nature that if it had not been well attested by witnesses worthy of credence I should hardly have dared to give it. In this connection, some time after the incident several Portuguese arrived at Zamora to be told of the incident which I am going to relate. Said one: "I will believe what you tell me when this boulder crumbles into pieces."

173

And he struck it with his foot. It did not actually crumble up but crashed and split in two pieces.

One day when the master was preaching to a great crowd he saw two criminals pass who were being led away to execution, their sentence being that of burning alive. He asked the officer in charge to allow them to wait while he finished his sermon, and such was the authority of the man that the officer obeyed and the two men were placed just beneath the platform on which Vincent was preaching, within hearing but out of sight of the auditors.

For three hours the master preached, first in general on sin and its punishment, stressing in burning words the offense and the infinite perfection of God Who is offended. Then he proceeded to speak more particularly of the men below him, using all the power of his matchless eloquence to paint their crimes against God and what depth of contrition, what desire of expiation should fill them.

The sermon ended, Vincent told the officer to fetch his charges. But, such was the effect of the word of truth on the poor sinners, such burning contrition did his words excite, such fires of remorse, that their bodies even had participated in the fiery sorrow of their souls and the officer found them lying just as they would have lain at the stake if the sentence had been carried out.

The number of the master's followers was always increasing. Colmenares, historian of Segovia, speaks of seventy to eighty thousand persons following him to hear his sermons. He had with him confessors for those who had been converted by his preaching, and lawyers to draw up the deeds of amnesty and amity which put an end to the bloody feuds which desolated so much of the country. He had also a properly constituted choir with minstrels and musicians to carry out the divine office with due solemnity.

# THE LAST PART OF THE SPANISH APOSTOLATE

When not far from Placensia, Vincent received a messenger from the Parliaments of Catalonia, Aragon and Valencia begging him to come as soon as possible to Caspe. The master set out immediately, for the question at issue was a very serious one. So that nothing might impede him, he avoided all large towns on his route, asking for the necessary hospitality in small villages and paying his debt by teaching them the word of God.

At Salanqua he determined to preach to the Jews, but as these would not come to him, he went to one of their synagogues. The Jews dared not turn out so celebrated a man, but his appearance caused a great tumult. When this had subsided the master began to preach, and as he spoke numbers of small white crosses appeared in the air and fell on the heads and clothes of the assembled Jews. The prodigy gave added weight to the preacher's words, and numerous conversions followed.

# Chapter XVII

## The Award of Caspe

We have followed our friar to the Papal court, to the
courts of kings; we have seen him among the magistrates of
innumerable cities, and preaching to masses of people both
lettered and unlearned. In each place his God-given wisdom
makes him the dominating personage; everywhere he is the
master. Now we find him a judge between kingdoms, playing a role which had far-reaching consequences, for the
future greatness of Spain was brought to birth by his choice.
In his hands lay the fate of a dynasty.

Henry the Sorrowful of Castile died leaving an infant
son, John II. The Estates of the Kingdom thereupon offered the crown to the late king's brother, the Prince of
Castile, Ferdinand d'Antequera, for it was not long since the
kingdom had suffered one disastrous minority and there was
no desire for another.

But the Prince would not accept what he considered by
right belonged to another, and entering the hall where the
Estates were assembled with his baby nephew carried high
on his shoulder, he cried aloud:

"Here is the King, my lords, who ought to reign. This child, the son of King Henry, my most honored brother, is your rightful Lord. For my part, I only ask the honor of being Governor of Castile until such a time as he is old enough to rule for himself. I invite you, then, in accordance with the laws and constitution of this kingdom, to tender him the Oath of Allegiance, and, according to the customary ceremonial, to accept him as your king."

And in his position as the first noble in the kingdom, Ferdinand knelt the first to pay homage to his infant nephew. Thus far the drama as it affected the Kingdom of Castile.

Aragon had been well and justly ruled by Martin the Humane, but he was now old and his only son had been killed fighting in Sardinia. It was a time of crisis, for the plague raged through the kingdom which was already rent by the Great Schism and by internal quarrels. Hoping against hope for an heir, the old king married Marguerite of Prades, young, beautiful, modest. But the union was without fruit, and the Cortes grew anxious for Martin to name an heir.

His personal inclination turned to his grandson Fadrique, the illegitimate son of his dead heir, and this young man had been recommended to Martin by the testament of the Crown Prince.

Another prince with a strong claim to the crown was Jaime, Count of Urgel. His father, Jaime, Count of Urgel, had been the second son of Jaime II, King of Aragon. The younger Jaime had married Isabella of Castile, his cousin, the daughter of a daughter of the same king. His father was dead, but his mother, an ambitious woman, gave her whole energies to fostering the same spirit of pride and ambition in her son. Goaded on by mother and son, the old king had made

Jaime Governor of Saragossa, a wise move inasmuch as Saragossa was the seat of furious and bloody factions, and the young man would have his hands full without furthering his personal ambitions; but unwise inasmuch as the Governorship of Saragossa also implied the succession to the throne.

Then sudden grievous illness struck the old king; the Cortes sent messengers to wait on him in Barcelona, begging him to settle once and for all the succession, but nothing definitive was arranged. Sometime previously, however, Martin had sent for his nephew, Ferdinand of Castile, telling him that he considered him as his nearest relative. So in accordance with his desires, Ferdinand had published an edict declaring that, "being the nearest relative of King Martin, he accepted the succession of all his kingdoms, lands and possessions, reserving to himself the right to put the declaration into effect at the proper time." Well did Ferdinand earn his title of "Just" and "Honorable"; having refused a throne to which, according to his conscience, he had not the first claim, he accepted that to which he had a right.

On the death of the king, the Cortes assembled at Catalonia in order to decide which claimant, in their opinion, had the best right of succession; and while the settlement was pending, they did all in their power to enforce order. They also invited plenipotentiaries from Aragon and Valencia to treat of a matter which was vital to the whole peninsula. But to wars and factions on all sides was added internal division in the Cortes itself. Finally the Catalans withdrew to meet at Tortosa, the State of Aragon at Alcaniz, while the Valencians actually held two opposing assemblies, one at Vinaroz and the other at Trayquera. In vain did the States of Catalona and Aragon send ambassadors to mediate, in vain did Benedict offer his intervention; there was nothing which could put an end to the scandal.

Then the opposing parties bethought them of Vincent Ferrer, and according to Curita: "In order to bring together so many opposing wills, so many incompatible sentiments, and an animosity so great that at any moment intrigue might break out in open warfare, all manifested a desire that the blessed Master, Vincent Ferrer, should be summoned to take part in the deliberations, since he was everywhere venerated for his sanctity of life, and his religious profession. Every kind of inducement was held out to him to persuade him to return, since he was the man who alone could put an end to such discord, particularly those dissensions which were the ruin of his mother-country, all being assured that, with such ministers, God was accustomed to work marvels."

Of the six candidates to the throne, the two whose right seemed clearest were: first, Ferdinand, Prince of Castile, chivalrous, disinterested, firm of purpose, a man who acted only after mature deliberation, solidly Christian, entirely honorable, and possessing fundamentally the confidence of the people; and Jaime of Urgel, beloved in Castile, liberal, simple in manner, and with a fine strong figure, but violent and unscrupulous, choosing his followers from among outlaws, and careless of the manner of persons with whom he allied himself, provided only that they furthered his ambitions.

As there seemed no possibility of reaching agreement, the Cortes finally decided to choose from the three Estates—ecclesiastical, noble and common—nine men known for their probity and impartial judgment, three to be chosen from each Estate. They were to deliberate at Caspe, a free city, under the jurisdiction of the Knights of Saint John of Jerusalem; no body of armed men was to come within a determined distance of the city. The majority necessary for a true election was to be six of the nine chosen electors. Among those chosen were one Archbishop, one Bishop, Boniface Ferrer, General of the Carthusians, and Vincent Ferrer of the Order of Preachers, his brother.

It is of interest as showing the universal esteem in which Vincent was held, to learn that after the choice of the electors, France at the instigation of the Duchess of Anjou accused Boniface Ferrer of partiality, thus invalidating his right of election. The ambassadors entrusted with this accusation offered to submit their contention before the other electors, specially Vincent Ferrer. They thus agreed to abide by the decision of one brother in regard to the other.

On the appointed day, the nine electors, after hearing Mass and communicating, took the following oath, with one hand on a book of the Gospels and the other on a Crucifix.

"I promise God, the Virgin Mary, and the whole celestial court, and I swear on the Cross of Jesus Christ and the holy Gospels, to proceed in the matter of the succession, and to make known the true Lord and King as soon as possible. In this matter I will act entirely according to God, justice and my conscience, putting aside all regard for affection, any petition made to me, any motive of fear or hatred, any hope of reward or favor, or any other unworthy motive. I further swear that I will neither manifest or make known in any way to anyone whatsoever other than to my fellow judges, directly or indirectly, by word, sign or writing, my wishes or my decision on this matter, nor the wishes or decision of the other judges until the day when this same decision shall be solemnly published."

The ceremony ended, Vincent was asked to preach, which he did on the text: "There shall be one fold and one shepherd," applying, with his customary clarity and felicity of expression, this text to the circumstances under which the electors had met.

After enumerating the nine choirs of angels he said:

"Souls, however, are gathered, some in the first choir, some in the second, and so on. . . . I will now tell you which souls belong to the first choir and which to the others. And whilst I am speaking, let each one of you consider if he follows such a manner of life as will permit him in heaven to join one of the heavenly choirs. There are in the world nine ways in which to live a good life, corresponding to the nine choirs of angels, and those who live the first grade of a good life will be gathered with the first choir of angels and so on.

*From the sermons; on rulers and ruling; given on the day of the election of the King of Aragon.*

"The sixth mode is better than the others, for it is that of Rulers (Dominations), whether ecclesiastical prelates or temporal rulers. This is a higher grade because it has respect, not only to the good of the person himself, but also to the good of the whole people subject to him. For he does not only rule himself well and virtuously, but also the whole people committed to him. Consider the blessing of good prelates, from the Pope to the parish priest, and from the Emperor to the city magistrate, when they hold their position by a just title. When such are in positions of command, they not only rule themselves according to the other five modes, but, furthermore, they rule the peoples with justice, because, neither love nor hatred, nor bribery tempts them to act contrary to justice; they are content with their just revenues and do not oppress their subjects. The same holds good with prelates who correct notorious vices; for secret sins do not come within the judgment of man but of God, and they are not to be punished either by the state or the communality.

181

"When such worthy rulers die, they are gathered with great rejoicing into the sixth choir, that of the Dominations. The Virgin Mary says to her Son: 'A great feast should be made, because in many years the like of this man has not ascended to heaven, because all have ruled themselves badly.'"

The electors then proceeded to hear the various claimants and their claims, a matter which occupied twenty days. When at last the deliberations were ended and the moment for decision arrived, the assembly asked Vincent to be the first to record his vote. After recollecting himself for a moment in silent prayer, he wrote: "I, Brother Vincent Ferrer, of the Order of Preachers, Master in Sacred Theology, one of the judges designated by the Cortes, affirm to the best of my knowledge that the aforesaid Cortes, the subjects and vassals of the crown of Aragon, owe fidelity to the most illustrious and magnificent lord, Ferdinand of Castile, kinsman of Peter, King of Aragon, of happy memory, who was father to the late most honored King Martin, since the said Ferdinand is his nearest male relative, issue of legitimate marriage; and I declare that, in strict duty, all ought to regard him as veritable King and Lord in justice; according to God and my conscience. In witness of which, I sign the present attestation with my own hand and seal."

Here is the account given of the event by an annalist of Aragon: "In my opinion it is a matter of high consideration that the holy man Vincent Ferrer was the first to cast his vote, although he found himself with men of such high dignity as the Archbishop of Tarragon, and the Bishop of Huesca, the most learned men of their time, and skilled in the study of civil and canon law. In a cause full of such inextricable difficulties complicated by different institutions involving the testaments of several kings, one substituted for the other, and being governed by the rights and customs of the country which have in such matters the force of law, men such as the archbishop and bishop are better qualified to prove their point than a religious who is only a theologian. But Our Lord willed it thus, in order to show more clearly that in this judgment He intervened, thus basing the judgment on something higher than reason, or the laws and customs of nations, and proving that reliance is not to be placed in knowledge and human wisdom only."

The Bishop of Huesca contented himself with subscribing: "In all and to the fullest extent, I adhere to the opinion of Master Vincent." Five others followed. The remainder, though differing in some points arrived at the same conclusion, and so Ferdinand, Prince of Castile, was elected King of Aragon.

Copies of the attestation were sent to each of the three Cortes, but the result of the election was kept inviolably secret until June 29, 1412, at nine o'clock in the morning, when the judges left the castle where they had remained throughout the deliberations. On a raised platform before the church, in the presence of the ambassadors of the three kingdoms, the nobility, and a huge concourse of people the Bishop of Huesca sang Mass. After the Mass, Master Vincent mounted the pulpit and preached on the text: "Let us rejoice and exult and give glory to God, because it is the nuptials of the Lamb." The interpretation of the text shewed that the Divine Will was manifested in all that had taken place. Then he read the Act of Election, for by common accord the judges had deputed him to be their mouthpiece.

As soon as the Act had been read, the other judges stood and cried aloud: "God save Ferdinand, our Lord and King!" And the whole waiting crowd took up the cry. Since, however, there were still some unsatisfied malcontents, the following day Vincent preached again, giving the history of the Congress and ending: "Leave to the evil-doers the responsibility of their own acts, and for your part do not despise the good will that God has manifested for you in this election."

That night Vincent left the castle to seek his own cell, and the next day he left Caspe to take up again his mission as Friar Preacher, and to continue his missionary journeys. He had only gone to the court of the King because God had called him, while there he had done his duty to his country, and now he took a route in the opposite direction to that taken by Ferdinand.

Jaime, Count of Urgel, was not the man to let a crown slip from his fingers without making every effort to regain it; when therefore Vincent heard that there was a possibility of civil war between the successful and unsuccessful claimants, he hastened to the King at Lerida, there to offer him all the support that his incomparable influence in the country afforded.

Jaime, however, had no intention of permitting the King to have his hand so greatly strengthened if he could prevent it. Accordingly he prepared an ambush in a lonely part of the road where he knew the master was bound to pass with a few of his followers. Springing out on Vincent, he seized him and, by way of prelude to more drastic action, he began to pour out his spleen in vituperation, calling the friar every evil name he could think of.

Vincent suffered this for a short while and then took him quietly aside to say in a low voice: "It is you who are the evil man; for in such a place on such a day and at such an hour you killed your brother. God did not wish to give the crown of Aragon to a criminal."

Overcome with amazement and fear at this revelation of something which he had believed known to himself alone, the count withdrew, leaving Vincent to go on his way in peace. So abashed was Jaime in fact, that but for a fresh intervention on the part of his mother, he would have made his submission to Ferdinand.

# Chapter XVIII

*Apostolic Journeys Recommenced*

Leaving the court of King Ferdinand, Vincent spent the summer and autumn of 1412 journeying along the east coast of Valencia. His chief work at this time was the reconciliation of enemies both public and private, and in this he was giving practical support to the new regime in whose inauguration he had had such a large share. A contemporary historian gives an account of his work in one town which may well serve as a picture of the whole.

"During the summer of 1412, the Apostle of Valencia, Vincent Ferrer, came to Castellon. At the time this town was at war with those of Oude and Alamnora, and the fighting was fierce and bloody. The saint brought to the task of peacemaking all the weight of his great eloquence, and profiting by the universal sympathy which was manifested for him, he put an end to even the most inveterate enmities. He addressed a discourse full of pathos to the magistrates of the three towns who had come together to one place for this end. Afterwards he persuaded them to

186

sign a Treaty of Peace before the Bailli General of Valencia whom he had summoned for this purpose. Everywhere his presence and preaching had the same effect. And so, at last there was a settlement of these interminable differences, which had caused such unrest and had embroiled the people in endless strife."

At Lucenia, acceding to the demand of the master, the magistrates framed two edicts: one against the quarrelsome habitues of the wine-shops, and the other putting a bound to the activities of the courtesans of the town. In order that there should be no excuse for ignorance or forgetfulness of these laws, the magistrates ordered them to be engraved on stone and placed in the most frequented part of the town.

Meanwhile, hearing that the King was at Lerida, Vincent made his way there. Here are the accounts of what followed, from more eye-witnesses:

"Jaime Quintanis, Master of Arts, and the King's doctor, heard about thirty of Master Vincent's sermons while he was at Lerida. Crowds thronged to hear him, and the enthusiasm of all, both men and women, was so great that they came at midnight to secure places for the following day. There had been in the town factions and inveterate enmities; and there seemed no hope of ending them on account of the many murders committed both on the one side and on the other. The salutary words of Master Vincent restored unity, peace and concord; all feuds were renounced; mortal enemies asked pardon one of the other and were publicly reconciled. All, both men and women, speaking many different languages understood Master Vincent as well as if he were speaking the idiom proper to

187

each, though in fact he spoke only in his mother tongue. After having heard such marvellous doctrine, full of practical lessons, a great number of persons, whose lives until that time had been one tissue of crimes, returned to God. Many embraced the religious life and made great progress therein. Many students of the different faculties in the University abandoned their careers to follow Master Vincent, the greater part of them having decided to live for worldly advancement no longer. In truth, it was often noticed that after he had been in a district, the monasteries and convents could not cope with the numbers of novices who presented themselves."

Once when Master Vincent was preaching in the square outside the Dominican Priory, in presence of King Ferdinand and a vast concourse of people, he saw about half a mile away, dragging himself towards the square, a sick man, so crippled that he was forced to crawl on all fours. Pausing in his sermon, Vincent addressed the King: "Your Majesty, I beg you, for the love of God, to send two of your grooms to that poor man over there, to find out if he is as crippled as he appears to be."

The King immediately dispatched two of his gentlemen, and when they reached the man, seeing that his condition was even more piteous than it had appeared at a distance, they made preparations to help him reach the preacher. As they stooped to lift him they glanced in the direction from which they had come to see the master make a large Sign of the Cross in their direction. Immediately the beggar rose, stood upright and began to walk as quickly and easily as if there were nothing the matter with him. The grateful man followed in the train of his benefactor for several years.

188

In another sermon the master painted such an accurate and telling picture of the effeminate, sensual lives of many young men about town that a young cleric, Laurence Peregrine, thinking with good reason that he was one of those to whom the preacher referred, left everything to become one of his most fervent disciples.

One day it happened that this convert, who had been given the charge of finding lodgings for the fraternity, was attacked by a bad bout of fever. Shivering and burning, he sought the master to tell him that he was unfit to carry out his charge.

"Go, all the same," answered the miracle-worker, "and by virtue of your obedience your fever will leave you."

In this connection a tale is told of one occasion when Vincent for once added a burden instead of giving relief; and this tale is also a striking testimony to the courage and virtue of the sufferer.

Urgent business had brought King Ferdinand to Lerida, but he was only able to remain there for a few days. He had come to receive the submission of the Count of Urgel, being immediately afterwards bound for Tortosa. But in spite of the pressure of business he did not intend leaving Lerida without seeing his confessor. Accordingly, one evening, he presented himself at the priory unannounced.

The brother who looked after the master and saw to his visitors took the King to Vincent's cell, but both were brought up short on the threshold. Absorbed in God, seeing and hearing nothing of what was going on around him, the friar knelt surrounded by a heavenly light. The King stood for a moment awe-struck, and then quietly left the cell without daring to address Vincent.

Next day, when the master heard of the occurrence, he was much displeased and did not hesitate to tell the King that he had acted most wrongly in using his prerogative to enter the convent precincts. As for the brother, for his share in acting as the King's guide, Vincent laid on him seven years of fever.

In spite of this affliction the brother had the courage and virtue to continue following him. Day after day he assisted at numberless miraculous cures, and while he himself shivered with fever, he listened patiently to the raptures and joyous blessings of those others who were so happily cured. At last, one day, when they had reached Vannes, he ventured to petition the master to forgive and deliver him.

"So be it," answered Vincent. "But hold yourself in readiness for you will die at the first hour on Sunday."

According to an eyewitness, when he was leaving Lerida, Vincent saw in the distance a great number of armed men. Turning to his companions he said: "Do you see those men coming? They are so enraged at the conversion of their light-of-loves, that they are coming to kill me."

"Let us defend you, then," answered those round him.

"No," said Vincent, "I command you to go on one side and leave me."

Vincent's followers, being convinced of their master's power over all sorts and descriptions of men, obeyed him, and the master advanced alone to meet the assassins. As they closed in on him, Vincent raised his hand and made a great Sign of the Cross. Immediately, the others laid down their arms, and kneeling at his feet, begged forgiveness. Then they joined themselves to the band already following the saint.

In March 1413, the master was back in Valencia, for the last time. Letter after letter reached him begging him to come and preach the Lent. And March 4th, the Saturday before Quinquagesima found him at the gates of his beloved native city, where a royal welcome awaited him. All the nobility were there in robes of state, all the clergy, all the religious of the place and the guilds. A magnificent canopy was held over Vincent on his little donkey, and there in the midst of this splendor he moved, rapt in God, thanking Him for His goodness, and making petition for the cloudy, dark future.

On arriving at Valencia, Vincent found himself once more in the cell he had occupied as a novice. The Duke of Gandia, who happened to be staying in the priory had been lodged in this cell as a signal mark of honor. Now the friars asked him to change it for another. They reckoned Master Vincent greater than even the Duke of Gandia, and they knew that no other lodging would be so pleasing to him.

The master preached this, his last Mission at Valencia, in an open square close to the cathedral. Miracles were not wanting. One was a striking commentary on vanity in dress. The dowager-queen, Marguerite de Prades, came to as many of Vincent's sermons as possible, accompanied by her sister Dona Juana. The latter affected great magnificence of dress, particularly in respect to hairdressing, for she wore her hair so high as to resemble a tower, encrusted in diamonds.

One day as she sat in her place, an enormous stone, falling from no one knew where, fell square on to this amazing erection. The members of the royal suite rushed at once to her, certain that she had suffered some terrible injury.

"No harm has been done," said Vincent dryly to the agitated bystanders. "That happened merely to discover if the tower was strong enough to withstand stones."

191

Another day, as he was passing down the street, the master was greeted by a perfect tornado of oaths, curses and blasphemies, and from one of the houses which stood on either side of the street, a man rushed out across the master's path and ran down the road, evidently beside himself with rage.

Vincent turned in at the open door to investigate, and found within a woman weeping vehemently and cursing fully as heartily as the man. She looked up as the master entered and wailed bitterly: "It is not only today, but every day that my husband beats me right well. I am covered with bruises and my life is a worse hell than if I were mated to the devil himself."

"There, that will do; that will do," responded Vincent. "Do not name that accursed name, for he comes only too quickly, even when he is not called. Be patient, and instead of swearing in this way which will only anger your husband still further, offer God your sufferings. Now, tell me pray, what is the cause of all this commotion?"

"It is," sobbed the woman, "because I am ugly."

"Is that all?" cried Vincent. "Can such a trivial matter lead to so much sin? But it can be remedied." And straightway he made her the most beautiful woman in all Valencia.

On another occasion, a woman came to seek Vincent, complaining bitterly of the brutality of her husband and begging for a secret remedy to restore peace to the house. Said Vincent, "Go and find the Brother Porter and tell him to give you a bottle full of water from the well in the cloister garden. As soon as your husband returns sip a mouthful at once and hold it in your mouth. Then you will very soon be the witness of marvels."

The woman did as she was bid, and not long after her return home her husband came back. He entered the room

192

where his wife was and immediately, according to custom, began to abuse her. But the woman's mouth being full of water it was out of her power to answer him back. Taken aback by her silence, the husband ceased his abuse; and being not a bad fellow at heart, he thanked God and praised the newly-found patience of his wife.

The latter, overwhelmed with joy at the turn events had taken and delighted with her husband's praise, hurried back to the friar to tell him of the miracle wrought by his remedy. Vincent smiled amusedly.

"The medicine I gave you," he told her, "was not the water from the well, which is no different from any other water, but silence. You were only making your husband more bad-tempered by your habit of answering him back. Your silence shamed him, soothed his anger, and gave him no excuse for abusing you. Keep silence on such occasions and you will always have peace."

At last the time came for Vincent to say a last farewell to his beloved native city. He spoke to the priory, the fatherland of his soul, as he stood at the door of his beloved cell and blessed the place where he had given himself to God and received the hundredfold.

"Console yourself," he said, "there will always be saints here"—a prophecy which has been realized in the event.

Then, one lovely July day, followed by the good-wishes of all, and accompanied by his usual following, Vincent left the city by the Reale Gate and set out for Barcelona.

The many followers of the master were a strange medley, and there were among them more than one simple, somewhat foolish soul, such as a certain young Lombard peasant. Hearing that there was but one thing necessary, he immediately left his village home and his fields to live as a hermit. But when Vincent passed through Lombardy, he turned his back on his hermitage to follow the master.

It happened that in the course of a sermon at Tray-guera on the way to Barcelona, Vincent chanced to refer to Saint Margaret who, feeble woman though she was, crushed the devil and held him for a long time under her foot. After the sermon the young Lombard withdrew to a solitary place and begged of God to allow the devil to appear to him, so that, after the example of Saint Margaret, he might fight and crush the fiend.

All on fire with his prayer he rose, and—lo and behold! —there stood before him a dirty little old woman, ragged and dishevelled, with dark wrinkled skin, a poor old villager who had been dumb from birth. In her hand she carried a sickle with which to cut the grass which grew thickly all round. The sudden apparition of this young man apparently rising from the ground frightened her, and she threatened him with her sickle.

"Ah-ha!" said the young man to himself, highly delighted. "My prayer has been answered and this is the devil in person, no possible doubt of it. Now it only remains for me to show myself as brave as Saint Margaret." Saying this, he flung himself on the old woman and threw her to the ground.

"Ah! cursed devil!" he cried, "you have had the better of me so often through invisible temptations, but now that I can see and take hold of you I will have my revenge." And full of his great purpose, he wrought so mightily with his hands and feet, that when he desisted to hurry away and give an account of his victory to the master, he left the poor old woman lying on the ground half dead.

But others of the villagers had seen what had happened and hurried off to the Alcaid, with the result that while the young man was in the midst of giving a triumphant account of his victory, he was seized and led away under guard to the magistrate.

But Vincent had gathered sufficient of the tale to remedy the trouble in his own fashion. Kneeling he prayed for a moment or two, then turning to one of his priests he said, "Go and hear the poor old woman's confession." "But she is dumb," chorused the bystanders.

"Do as I have told you," persisted the master. He was obeyed and the poor old woman made her confession quite distinctly, retaining the gift of speech for as long as she lived. As for the young athlete, he was sent back to his fields.

At the end of August, in response to many appeals, Vincent visited the island of Majorca, setting sail from Barcelona in company with the bishop of the place. The welcome he received was truly royal.

According to the historian, Mut, each evening he organised a procession of flagellants, when the tears of all witnessed to the fervor that he was able to inspire. At the time of his arrival there had been a drought for some time, but from the third day of his preaching abundance of rain fell on the whole island. The grateful people followed him everywhere. Although the church of the Dominicans was immense it was not large enough to hold the steadily increasing crowd. So the wall of the Friars' garden was pulled down, and a large platform built so that the preacher could be seen by all. People could hear him from the distance of three leagues, and though he spoke in Valencian, all could understand him. He remained in the island for nearly half a year.

When in early February he was ready to embark again, all the people brought provisions for him and his following. On the quayside he asked a wine-seller to sell him some wine, and the man agreed.

"Tip up your wineskin," commanded Vincent, holding his scapular in the form of a cup between his two hands.

"But you will get yourself badly stained," said the by-standers.

"Do not be afraid," answered Vincent. Accordingly the wine-seller emptied his skin into the scapular, and the water, which according to the custom of such folk, was liberally mingled with the wine, remained in the scapular, while the modicum of wine filtered through. There was a good laugh at the expense of the vendor.

During his sojourn at Majorca, he preached in each place where he stopped three or four sermons on the Last Judgment. Often enough he preached three or four times in one day. The miracles which he worked are countless, especially in regard to possessed persons. The Majorcan friar who cut Vincent's tonsure, kept some of the hair which he cut off, and after the Master's departure, this continued to work miracles for the cure of the possessed.

A letter from King Ferdinand recalled Vincent to Tortosa.

# Chapter XIX

*The Conference at Tortosa*

While he was at Majorca, Vincent received the following letter from King Ferdinand.

"Our beloved and devoted Religious,

" . . . For the rest, beloved and devoted friend, there are in our realm many children of Moses, ensnared in the toils of Judaism, whose hearts inspired by the Grace of the Holy Spirit, long with ardor to take flight into the shelter of the Catholic Faith. They are thirsting to be helped by the instruction of some understanding person, whose instructions may bring them where their unaided grasp of religion is not strong enough to lead them.

"Since we hope that the brightness of your edifying sermons may bring them out of the darkness in which they now live to the light of the Catholic Faith, we lovingly request you and exhort you in the Lord as soon as you read these presents to repair without delay to Tortosa, where many Jews for the aforesaid reason are gathered together, that from you these same Jews may gather the palm of salvation, so that they may be enabled to enjoy eternal life in Heaven. From there we hope you will go to Saragossa, where, God willing, we propose to celebrate in a short time our solemn coronation, that, by your saving presence, as many Jews as possible may forsake their Jewish religion for the joy of the true Faith. We have written to the royal Procurator that all that is necessary for you and your followers may be prepared as soon as possible. Given at Illerda under our secret seal November 20, 1413.

"Ferdinand the King"

This letter was sufficient to ensure Vincent's immediate departure from Majorca. All through his missionary career he had worked indefatigably for the conversion of the Jews and his success had been very great. This fact was regarded by many of his own time as one of the signs of the approaching end of the world.

Benedict had been in communication with one of Vincent's most famous Jewish converts, the Talmudist, Josue Halorqui, who had been baptised by the Master at Alcaniz. The Pontiff had received from him proposals that a conference should be held at Tortosa between himself and the chief Rabbis. Josue stated that he intended basing his arguments not on the Bible but on the Talmud itself; therefore, since Halorqui was himself a recent convert, Benedict judged it more prudent to postpone the conferences until the arrival of Vincent.

The master arrived in Tortosa about January 20, 1414, and set to work immediately in preparation for the conferences. His night watches brought to birth "The Treaty against the Jews" which is now preserved in the Vatican archives; according to Père Fages, it is the best of its kind ever written. It is prefaced: "Here begins a new and exceedingly compendious tract against the perfidy of the Jews. It was compiled and brought out on the order of Benedict the Pope so called by those under his obedience, by four famous masters in Sacred Theology, of whom one was Brother Vincent Ferrer. Among the collaborators were Jerome de Saint-Foi, physician to Benedict and converted by Vincent Ferrer, and his almoner Andrew Bertrand, who afterwards became Bishop of Barcelona."

Jerome de Saint-Foi was the name taken in Baptism by Halorqui.

The conference opened on February 7th under the presidency of Benedict himself, and all the later sessions were presided over by the Master General of the Dominicans. To the conference were gathered the chief Rabbis of the kingdom and the principal Catholic theologians, the leader of whom was Vincent Ferrer. A sort of agony of doubt possessed the Jews at this time. They were drawn to Christianity almost against their wills and so they remained poised between the old and new dispensations, not knowing which way to turn. Vincent, knowing this, knew also the best way to help them; and they realising that the friar understood their difficulties turned to him in their anguish. The results of this foreknowledge were sometimes astonishing.

On one occasion he was preaching on the far side of the river, from a house situated in a grove of trees. An immense multitude was gathered to hear him. Suddenly in the midst of the sermon, the preacher stopped and looked upwards.

"Do not be annoyed at this delay," he said after a few moments. "I must await on Grace."

Vincent stood in silence, while the crowd, hushed and expectant, began to move, shifting little by little until a clear space was left round the pulpit. Soon down the road there appeared a party of Jews, strangers whom no one was expecting. These came forward and without hesitation moved to the space from which the crowd had drifted, and so stood right below the pulpit.

The sermon ended, the bystanders began to question them as to what had brought them.

"We do not know," they answered, "we can only tell you that we felt a sudden inspiration which we obeyed." On that day and the next great numbers of Jews were converted.

The conference held sixty-nine sessions, and lasted until the November of that year. Each of Vincent's sermons roused violent dissension among the Rabbis; there were heated discussions, but in the end truth prevailed over the greater number. Forty Rabbis, not counting their followers, abjured their errors, Master Astruc Levi making the abjuration in the name of the rest.

This mass conversion had one unforeseen result. The consequent cessation of usury allowed of better conditions among the agricultural communities. Harvests were not impounded beforehand to pay old debts, and so prices were lower.

The first part of the year 1415 was taken up with fresh journeyings, this time through Aragon. Their history is a familiar one: miracles, preaching, conversions. At Cervera, however, a prodigy of a different kind took place. While Vincent was resting one night in a priory of his Order, the ceiling of his cell opened to permit the entrance of the radiant figure of Saint Dominic, who had come to seat himself in a fatherly fashion at the side of the plank bed of his son. Vincent would have risen to kiss the Father's feet.

"No," said Saint Dominic, "you are my well-beloved son, and I wish to talk to you as father to son."

Among other things, Saint Dominic assured Vincent of his eternal salvation. As time went on the conversation grew more and more animated, continuing until morning. The unaccustomed sound of voices drew the attention of the other friars; they went to the door of the cell, but there stopped short, awed to see rays of light coming through the crack in the door.

The next morning, Vincent was questioned, and to prevent the tale getting abroad, under promise of secrecy he explained exactly what had happened.

Almost daily during the journey through Aragon, food and drink were miraculously multiplied to serve the needs of those who followed the master.

# Chapter XX

## *The Evangelization of the Midi*

Vincent Ferrer did not attend the Council of Constance. Although asked to do so by Alphonso, the young King of Castile, and by Gerson who wrote begging him to come in the name of the Council, the master felt that his work with regard to the schism was completed, and that he must now carry out the orders of Christ Himself, to preach repentance and the approach of the Judgment. So for the last time he left Spanish soil, saying good-bye to the Fatherland, for his bones were to rest in that peninsula which stretches out into the Atlantic, looking towards the yet undiscovered New World, truly for him the ends of the earth.

France needed the master. Two years previously Henry V of England had invaded France, and everywhere his armies were victorious. The country itself was divided in its adherence between the Armagnacs and the Burgundians, and it was this state of civil war which had rendered possible the invasion of the country by its English enemies.

Before his death, Vincent again took some part in the temporal affairs of the kingdom, but now his first objective was the conversion of the people. Very full accounts are available of his stay in the various cities of the Midi; but, to avoid monotony, it will suffice to take the witness of Saint Dominic's own city of Toulouse, for what occurred there also took place in countless other cities of the realm.

On the Friday before Palm Sunday, Vincent Ferrer entered the city, a bent old man, riding on an ass harnessed with a pack saddle, without bridle, and the stirrups no more than wooden blocks fastened to the saddle by pieces of cord.

He made his entry betwen four and five in the evening, a great multitude of people going before him. He intended going to the priory of the Dominicans, but the crowd in the square was so compact that he had to betake himself to the house of the parish priest. He stayed there for some time, but even when he emerged, the mass of people was so dense that the authorities were obliged to surround him by a barricade of planks carried by strong men, before, behind and on either side of the ass. Otherwise he would have been crushed by the hundreds who pressed on him to kiss his hands. Even as it was, the folk, determined not to be balked of their desire for some commemoration of him, threw their handkerchiefs in his direction as he passed.

And so it was, right through his stay in the city. The sacristan of the priory, although he always opened the church door very early, invariably found there a crowd who, in order to hear the sermon, had been patiently waiting for six or seven hours.

One morning the sacristan forgot to open the door as early as usual and by the time he remembered it the press of people was so great that a woman who fell was trampled on by more than a hundred persons. Badly crushed, but still conscious, she invoked Vincent and found herself able to rise, and stumble in to Mass and the sermon. At its conclusion, she suddenly found herself completely restored, and without pain or other trace of the accident.

At first Vincent refused to work miracles in public, wishing to avoid any temptation to vainglory. But when he saw the disappointment of the people, his tender heart could not hold out against them and he began his daily work of blessing the sick and laying his hands on them.

This is the witness of Bernard de Rosergio, the Archbishop of Toulouse:

"He preached for six days in the cloister of the Dominican convent, but the crowds who flocked to hear him were so great that he was given a platform suitably placed before the Cathedral.

"After singing Mass, Master Vincent began his sermon, his face lit and his whole physiognomy that of a young man. His words were penetrated by such ardent charity, his tone vibrated so strongly, and he explained the sacred Mysteries with such enthralling eloquence that his auditors, learned or simple, listened entranced to him, receiving food for their souls and giving not the slightest sign of fatigue or boredom, although the sermon always lasted for at least three hours. Everyone in the city and its neighborhood, ecclesiastics and seculars, hastened to hear him; it made no difference whether the day were a public holiday or no, all work was suspended, the law-courts were closed, shops, workshops, inns, the offices of public officials, no business was carried on anywhere."

Daily while Vincent Ferrer stayed in the episcopal palace, there came a great crowd of sick of every age and condition. Then Master Vincent left his room and, his hands joined on his breast, addressed them with words of consolation, exhorted them to put all their confidence in God, and made the Sign of the Cross over them saying: "Jesus, Son of Mary, Master and Salvation of the world, be propitious and merciful to them." Then he blessed each in turn with the same invocation. Sometimes he laid his hand on their heads, blessing them on the forehead, and many affirmed that after this they felt themselves cured of their diseases. On Holy Thursday he cured a paralytic before the people.

He brought rain or made it cease at will; he did this in the cathedral square; he did it in the court of the Carmelite convent, where he gave a little lesson to the impatient crowd.

"Come my good people! It is only water, not stones; and in any case, God will provide." Then in response to a Sign of the Cross, the clouds parted in two, just as one might make a rent in a piece of cloth.

On Good Friday, Master Vincent preached in the presence of the Archbishop, a great number of Masters of Sacred Science, Doctors and Licentiates of Canon and Civil Law, royal officers, and a crowd of thirty thousand people. His sermon was on the Passion, and he represented in so lively a manner, in accents so sorrowful, the cruelty of the Jews, that everyone felt as though he or she were assisting at the reality of the tragedy. Pity and contrition drew tears from all. The sermon lasted for six hours without anyone showing the least fatigue.

Space does not permit the reproduction of the notes of the whole, but the touching introduction gives some faint idea at least of its beauty and pathos:

205

ANGEL OF THE JUDGMENT

*From the sermons; given on Good Friday at Tou-louse, in 1416; on the Passion.* "During this entire week we have made daily repre-sentation and memorial of the Passion of Jesus Christ. To-day we make this representation in a very different fashion. Until now it has been brought before us as something long since past, and therefore in the Mass the Gospel began 'At that time'; but today the Gospel begins as though we were speaking of some thing actually present before us. 'Jesus went out.' And the reason for this is that something pres-ent moves the hearts of men much more deeply than any memory of the past. The minute prick of a fly's sting is more painful at this moment than is the healed scar of an old wound. And so that we may feel the sweetness and may suffer in our own souls the death of Christ, let us represent it today as though it were actually occurring in our midst. This is what is done in the Office of the Church, which speaks as though Christ were actually to be seen on the cross, in order that we may experience the words of Lamentations: 'I will remember my poverty and trans-gression, the wormwood and the gall.'

"Thus speaks Christ, and the prophet answers in the person of the Christian people: 'These things I will re-member in my heart.'

" 'Remember' that is the past, but 'I will' that is the present, therefore this word is as though I were saying: 'Let us speak as though we saw Jesus crucified.' Let us also see the dolors of the Blessed Virgin Mary as though they were present before us. Now, you know that no salutation is made to a sorrowful person, not does one dare to speak in a joyful manner to one weighed down with sadness. Therefore today we cannot salute her in the ac-customed manner, because her soul is so full of sorrow that she might say: 'How can you say Hail to me who am so full of bitterness and sorrow and misery?' If we say: 'The

206

Lord is with thee,' she may answer: 'The Lord is not with me, for they have taken Him away and crucified Him.' If we call her 'Blessed' she may say: 'How can you call me blessed when all are speaking evil of me?' And therefore today we will not salute her. But, lest we should preach without devotion, let us turn to our crucified Lord hanging on the Cross and say: 'We adore thee, O Christ, and we bless thee because by thy holy cross thou hast redeemed the world.' "

On that Good Friday, many had come from a great distance to hear so famous a preacher. He spoke, as always, in the Valencian tongue. Nevertheless, everyone understood him as perfectly as though he had been a compatriot of their own.

Whilst he was preaching, a young man fell from a high place and was grievously hurt. The preacher cured him immediately and returned at once to his sermon, but the enthusiasm of the people was greater than their reverence for a holy place, and they raised a great cry: "A prophet has arisen up amongst us, and God has visited his people."

For a moment the preacher was silent, then demanding renewed attention by a gesture of his hand, he continued his discourse with such efficacy of grace that he was again interrupted by groans, sobs and other signs of grief and penitence. No one left him unless he were contrite and changed in heart, because he spoke the word of life in an accent which had been unknown since the days of the Apostles.

On the previous Palm Sunday Vincent had preached in the church of Saint Stephen, on the text, "Arise ye dead and come to Judgment." He struck such terror in the hearts, souls, and even the senses of those who were listening to him that he seemed more than a mere man, and rather an angel calling humanity to the supreme tribunal. Several times during the sermon the immense crowd which filled not only the nave of the church but the square outside and the surrounding streets, fell prostrate, more than one crying aloud on God for mercy.

So great was the success of his mission that every public sinner was converted. After his first sermon, the courtesans came in tears to give the keys of their houses to the town officials. Little by little all gambling and blasphemy ceased entirely.

Said Jean Inardi, one of the royal judges: "This man came to save us. Up to this time it was possible for us to plead ignorance, but what can we say after having heard such a preacher? If we do not listen and amend our lives we are lost. I know for certain of many people who before had tried in vain to fight against sensuality and luxury, but after having heard him, they entirely corrected themselves. I have heard the Archbishop of Toulouse, a brilliant theologian, say that since the apostle Paul, the Church has never had a preacher comparable to Master Vincent."

There were episodes which might have ended unpleasantly, but in the event they only redounded to the glory of the master. A young man who was perched high up over the west door of the church, and consequently behind the master, fell asleep in this very unsafe position. The crowd watching how he lurched and swayed, were so distracted that they began to cry aloud. Vincent half turned very quietly and made the Sign of the Cross. The young man awoke at once and removed himself to a safer coign of vantage.

One day an unmannerly religious interrupted the orator in the midst of a discourse on the end of the world.

208

"But, Father," he cried, "it is written that before the end of the world Babylon will be destroyed." After the bystanders had fruitlessly endeavored to make him hold his peace, Vincent Ferrer answered him. He said: "Without any doubt Babylon will be destroyed. But you must understand the sense of the words. Babylon means 'confusion of sin,' or if you prefer it, 'the world-wide disorder through sin.' "

At Toulouse, Vincent had marvellous success in inspiring the spirit of penance. Numbers of people gave themselves to the public processions of the discipline. In the evening they went through the town in bands, chanting plaintive hymns in honor of the Passion.

The notary Hugues writes: "I was one of those who organized the processions of the flagellants. It was impossible not to see the direct action of God as one watched these notabilities, clergy and laity publicly performing this act of penance. The processions took place in the evenings, and in order not to be recognised, the disciplinanti clothed themselves in the obscurity of a sort of tunic of linen reaching to their feet, opened only at the back from the neck to the waist-belt. I have seen them thus to the number of two or three hundred."

These processions continued long after the departure of the friar. They took place both on feasts and on ferias.

That these public acts of penance were no mere emotional outburst caused by the excitement of Vincent's presence is proved by the fact that after his departure, the Toulousains made another procession of reparation to a place called Cofeltra, where formerly they had met for disgraceful orgies and travesties of religious observance. There, in the church, where formerly there had been shows of all sorts of mimes and jugglers, now the same

209

people marched processionally, preceded by a great wooden cross, and scourging themselves as they went.

Vincent made his way by slow stages to Besançon, for while still at Saragossa he had promised to go there to meet Saint Colette, the Poor Clare. On reaching the city he went straight to her convent, and remained there for some time in private conference before going to his own priory in the town. He preached six times in the conventual church of Saint Clare before Colette and her companions.

We do not know the subject of the conversations held between the two saints; we only know that six weeks after Vincent left Besançon the Fathers of the Council of Constance received a joint letter from the two, telling them, on the part of God, that if they held firm, they would elect a great Pope who would end the schism and restore peace.

Speaking one day with Colette's confessor, Vincent told him that he had come from Spain into France in order to see her, for one day while he was at prayer in Saragossa, he saw Colette in prayer at the feet of Jesus Christ, imploring him to end the schism and to show mercy to the sinners who were the cause.

"Jesus Christ gave me to understand," added the master, "that it was His will that I should go to Besançon to see her, preaching meanwhile in the towns of France, and that while I was with Colette at Besançon He would communicate to us His designs in as far as they had respect to the interests of the Church."

On her side, Colette told Vincent that it had been revealed to her that God would call His servant to Himself in less than two years, as a recompense for his great services.

"In less than two years?" repeated Vincent in astonishment. "I trust that Our Lord will allow me to die in Spain."

"Not in Spain, in France," answered Colette, and her prophecy was fulfilled to the letter.

On Wednesday, June 9th, Vincent entered Dijon, and during his sojourn there an assembly arrived from the Council sitting at Constance. There was a difficult point on which the Fathers could not agree, and the Dominican Master General, Jean dePuynoix, suggested referring it to Vincent. "He will tell us the truth, for never has a lie been found on his lips." So they sent Cardinal Sant-Angelo, two Masters in Theology and two Doctors.

When the difficulty was laid before him, Vincent said: "You cannot find a solution because, on account of the pride of some of those at the Council, God has refused to enlighten you. This matter is mere child's play, and I am amazed that so many learned men have been unable to reach a solution." And he proceeded to elucidate the matter.

The ambassadors returned to the Council with the answer which was so perfectly lucid that they were unable to improve on it by one word. "A word from this man," it was said, "carried more weight than those of all the learned Cardinals and Doctors sitting in the Council."

While Vincent was at Auvergne, John, Duke of Brittany, sent three letters to him begging him to come to Brittany to re-establish the Faith. After reading the letters, in all good-will and humility Master Vincent consented to travel to Brittany.

# Chapter XXI

## *At the Ends of the Earth*

Vincent was now an old man. All through his life he
had used himself to the utmost limit of his powers; he had
given God everything and never had his body received
mercy. Now, when that obedient body was almost spent
he was called to Brittany.

His followers watched him with loving anxiety, and
seeing how feeble and spent he was, when the party
reached Nantes, they begged him to go no further, but to
return to Valencia, there to end his days in the priory of his
native city where he was professed. All God's gifts are a
fulfilling; they widen instead of narrow, and so sanctity
—love of God—does not preclude earthly love, and human
love is most noble when it is expended on parents and
country. So Vincent, who appears to have forgotten Saint
Colette's prophecy, listened to his friends and telling no one,
for fear of saddening the good people of Nantes, set out by
night on his return journey.

All night the party travelled, the feeble old master
riding his little she-ass. But when morning dawned, to the

212

unbounded surprise of all, the cavalcade found that they were still at the gates of the same city.

Said Vincent: "God wills that I die here in Brittany." And passing through the town, he began to make his way towards Vannes. And because age had so completely exhausted him, the duchess sent her litter to bring him. At Vannes he was to die.

Vincent entered the city on the Saturday before Laetare Sunday in the year 1418. The bishop and chapter, the clergy, the local nobility and the people marched to meet and escort him into Vannes. In the public square he was given a magnificent reception. He must have refused the proffered litter of the duchess, for we are told that he was still mounted on his donkey, and that he went thus to the house of Robin-le-Scarb where he lodged.

This public entry was, like every other, a curious study in contrast. On the one hand there were the greatest figures in the land, headed by the Duke and Duchess of Brittany; but on the other, when he reached the city gates, there, waiting in two lines, were the sick and the deformed, the cripple and the paralytic, folk covered with hideous sores, all waiting for the blessing of the master. It is difficult to conceive the enthusiasm, the delirium of the multitude when, by the power of this benediction, they saw bent backs straighten, the blind look round with flashing eyes, cripples discard their crutches, pushing to one side the little carts in which they had been wheeled. There the cripple and the paralytic stood upright and strong, lifting loosened arms to heaven. Then they all walked in the forefront of the cortege, praying and singing, with sonorous voices echoing from a full heart.

Among the sick was a man so paralyzed that he had no power of movement whatever. Seeing the other sick return-

213

ing cured while he himself was unable to make the slightest movement in the direction of the Master, the poor man began to cry as loud as he was able: "O Servant, O Friend of God! Deign to hear me." And over and over again, "Have pity on me, great servant of God!"

Touched with pity, Vincent passed close to the paralytic, saying as he did so in the words of the Apostle Peter: "Silver and gold I have none; but what I have I give thee. In the Name of Jesus Christ, get up and return to your house."

So saying, he laid his hands on the sick man with his customary formula, and immediately the sick man rose, completely cured. The master's eyes filled with tears as he said aloud: "To thee, O Lord and to Thy holy Name, be all glory and honor."

The man on whom the miracle had been worked could hardly obey the master's orders to return to his house through the excited throngs who pressed on him.

The next day—Laetare Sunday—Vincent preached in the presence of the whole ducal court on the text, "Gather up the fragments lest any be lost." The sermon is extant, and it is worth while quoting some extracts of this, the last sermon whose text we know, since it breathes the gentle charity, the loving comradeship and the sanctity of the old man.

*From the sermons; given on Laetare Sunday at Vannes, in 1418; on the text, "Gather up the fragments lest any be lost."*

"The holy Gospel read today on which I am going to preach makes mention of that solemn banquet which our Father Jesus Christ (*Papa Jesus Christus*) made in the desert. It is called great, first in respect to Him who made it, Christ; secondly in respect to those invited, the Apostles and many others; thirdly, in respect of what they had to eat; and fourthly, in respect to the multitude. But we were not worthy to be present at this banquet, to eat of this

214

wonderful bread. And although it is now a long while since that banquet was held, there still remain some fragments for us in the Gospel story.

"This was why Christ said: 'Gather up the fragments that are left over and above.' It is thus that a great Lord would speak to his servants after he has dined, and since they were not at the meal they search eagerly on the table afterwards. This table is the Gospel story. Let us gather up what we can find from this table; we shall have six morsels. First, penitential observance; second, intellectual prudence; third, regular ordinance; fourth, divine confidence; fifth, liberal mercy; sixth, virtuous benevolence.

"The first morsel which we must pick up is penitential observance, that is, penance for sin. The table from which we take it is the Gospel story: 'Jesus went across the sea of Galilee which is Tiberias and there followed him a great multitude, because they saw the signs which he wrought on the sick. Jesus therefore went up into the moutain and sat there with his disciples. Now the Pasch, the festival day of the Jews was at hand.' Let us see if in these words we may find some morsel of good bread. . . . Great crowds followed Him for several reasons.

"The first and best reason is that of love. In the second place there is devotion to Jesus Christ and His words, surely no surprising reason, for those words issued from the mouth of the Word Incarnate, of sweet savor in the hearts of men. Others followed by reason of bodily necessity, because He cured them by word or touch just as He pleased. And this third reason is continued in the text: 'A great multitude followed Him because they saw the signs that He wrought on them that were diseased.' Others again followed Him from mere worldly curiosity that they might witness these same miracles. Others, in fine, like the pharisees, followed

Him from devilish malignity, that they might find something to reprehend in Him. And so a great multitude followed Him. . . . And Jesus sat on the mountain.

"Let us see whether we can find some morsels for ourselves? And indeed we may well do so, for if we open the table-napkins we shall find penitential observance or penance. The Gospel tells us that Jesus Christ crossed the sea and afterwards rested on the mountain. Sea signifies penance, because 'mare' is derived from 'amaritudo,' bitterness. Now every act of penance is bitter, for in it contrition holds the first place; and contrition is bitter for it is none other than sorrow for past sins. In the second place penance implies the resolution to sin no more, and this is bitter inasmuch as it contradicts evil customs. In the third place confession is bitter, for it is bitter that the confessor who thought you were virtuous should know your shamelessness and wickedness. In the fourth place is affliction, such as works of penitence. Prayer also may be bitter, for he who prays is like one being racked, for his hands are raised high above his head and his body is dragged downwards with heavy stones. The body is this stone, as we read in the Book of Wisdom: 'For the body which is corruptible is a load upon the soul; and the earthly habitation presseth down the mind that museth upon many things. . . .' As Isaias says: 'Behold in peace is my bitterness most bitter.' Bitterness of heart by contrition; greater bitterness of the mouth by confession; greatest bitterness in the body making satisfaction. Behold then the sea.

"But those who cross the sea with Christ gain the ascent of the mountain, for otherwise, except by penance, we dare not climb. So you see the morsel of penance, of which David asks in the Psalm: 'Who shall go up to the mount of the Lord, or who shall stand in the holy place?' He answers: 'The innocent of hands and clean of heart. . . .' The first way is by alms, the second by restitution of ill-gotten goods and the third is by asking forgiveness. And they who act thus are the innocent of hands and clean of heart. . .

"Here is the second morsel of bread—intellectual prudence—when Christ, the Eternal Wisdom, sought counsel of Philip who was simple and dull that we may the more easily learn to seek counsel from simple folk. . . . It once happened that a certain master skilled in theology could not understand a phrase of Scripture, so he fasted and prayed but no enlightenment came to him, until he decided to humble himself and ask help from another. Then an angel appeared and explained the difficulty most fully. And therefore, when, for the sake of humility you reveal your thoughts to another, God will illuminate your mind and your doubts will be resolved. This is the second morsel, intellectual prudence.

"The third morsel is regular ordinance. . . . If you ask why Jesus did not will that the multitude should eat until they were all arranged in order, since that meant a considerable delay, I answer that in this napkin is hidden the third morsel, since, if we wish God to provide for the community it must be well ordered. . . . Blessed therefore is that Christian, that religious, that priest or any other, whose whole time is well ordered; God will provide for them.

"The fourth morsel is confidence in God, in all our difficulties or necessities, because, though friends and relations may lack money, God is never lacking in necessaries. . . . For when Jesus Christ saw the multitude in order, He took the bread and the fishes and holding them in His hands, with eyes raised to heaven, He blessed and gave them to His disciples and His disciples gave them to all the rest, until everyone was satisfied and still the food multiplied. And this was done in three ways: First as it was broken in the hands of Our Lord; in the second way it was multiplied in the arms of the Apostles; thirdly, between the teeth of those who were feeding. See how it was multiplied and they were filled. And as to its delicious taste, I tell you that no bread was ever before so sweet and full of flavor, for it is a rule of theology that whatever Jesus did miraculously was far better than anything which befell in the course of nature, as, for instance, those who received their sight, or their health, and when water was made wine at the marriage feast of Cana. . .

"The next morsel is confidence in God. When the Apostles were in despair because they could not provide food for the multitude, Christ wished to provide it in an unusual way so that we may realise that, however desperate the situation may appear we must never despair of God's help but have great confidence, not following the farmers who say: 'If it does not rain we shall have no grain this year.' For such have no confidence in God nor a right intention, for God can give not only wheat in the fields, but even in the granaries. The same holds good with regard to wine or anything else. That He does not give it is due to our lack of confidence.

"It happened once in the city of Valencia that, when the wheat was two hand-spans above ground there came a terrible drought, and the grain grew no higher. Numberless processions were made with many litanies, but no rain fell. When harvest time came, the folk reaped these miserable little stalks of grain, and never before had they such a harvest, never before had the heads been so full of grain. Granted, there was little straw, but that did not matter. And so if we follow Christ He will provide for us. . .

218

"And it is pleasing to God that we should speak of Him, like a small boy speaks of his father. For, if you ask a child, 'What are you going to eat today?' he will say, 'My father will see to that.' If you ask him, 'When your clothes are worn out who will give you others?' he will answer, 'My father will see to that.' This is the way in which God wishes us to treat Him, to have the same confidence in Him as a child has in his human father. But we have less confidence in God than in a Jew or a Moor: for if you have a properly signed deed of gift or sale by which a Jew is obliged to pay you twenty or thirty florins, and if I were to ask you, 'How are you going to get corn this year?' you would answer, 'Such a man is under obligation to me.' And you do not put your trust rather in God. You do God an injury because He has drawn up for you, by the trustworthy notary, Matthew, a deed of promise: 'Seek ye first the Kingdom of God and his justice and all these things shall be added to you.' And again: 'Be not solicitous saying: What shall we eat or drink or wherewith shall we be clothed? For after these things do the heathens seek. For your Father knoweth that you have need of these things!' Confide therefore in God as your Father, and seek His honor and justice, that is by sorrow for sins and confidence in Him. This then is the morsel of bread, Confidence in God. And therefore Christ willed to feed the multitude in this unaccustomed fashion."

Daily the master preached from the fourth Sunday in Lent until the Tuesday in Easter week, and after the sermon he cured the sick who came to ask his help.

After twenty-four days spent at Vannes, on the Tuesday in Easter week in the year 1418, Vincent left the city to evangelize the rest of Brittany. He had just one year to live. His mission through the duchy was of a piece with the rest of his journeyings, daily sermons to huge crowds of people, followed by miracles without number; and everywhere there were conversions, feuds ceased, quarrels were ended, breaches were healed, and there was a general reform of manners.

Henry V, King of England, having come to Normandy, was wishful to hear for himself that irresistible voice imprisoned in such a feeble body, so he sent a message by herald, requesting the master to come and preach to him.

The ambassador found the friar at Rennes, preaching to a congregation of thirty thousand persons. After listening to the sermon, he gave his message and Vincent, hoping by this means to bring about peace between the countries of France and England, set out at once, followed by the major part of those who had listened to him at Rennes.

Henry was at Caen, and thither Vincent made his way. At Saint-Lo a boy ten years old was brought to the master by his parents to be cured. This child was suffering from a strange and mysterious malady, so that at last he could neither eat nor drink, though, strange to say, he continued to grow. He heard and understood what was said to him, as was evident by his expression, but he was incapable of making any sort of response, even by a sign. The master listened to the parents' petition, he saw the child, but refused to do anything for him then and there.

"Bring the child to Caen," he said. So the parents joined the procession following the friar, wheeling the child in a little hand-cart.

On reaching Caen, the friar was conducted to a great open space, where the king was seated in state surrounded by his officials and the leaders of his army, while a huge multitude stood on the outskirts. As soon as the sermon was ended, the parents of the sick boy, fearing that they would be forgotten among the crowd, pushed their way with the cart to the front near the master, begging piteously that he would intercede for their son, and obtain either a cure or a speedy death.

Vincent looked at the pleading parents, then turning to the bystanders he told them to pray.

When the multitude was in prayer, the master made the Sign of the Cross over the child saying: "May the Blessing of God, Father, Son and Holy Ghost descend on thee and remain forever." Next he spoke to the boy himself: "My child, what do you want of God?"

"Father," answered the sufferer, "I desire the good pleasure of God which is being accomplished at this moment." Then he asked for food and drink, and there, before the eyes of all, he ate a hearty meal. And this inaugurated his complete recovery.

This is the witness of the boy himself as a man of forty-six years.

"I had been in this state for seven years; Master Vincent had come to preach in Normandy. I was shown to him first at Saint-Lo, but he would do nothing for me there, and commanded my parents to bring me to Caen, where the King of England and his suite were in residence. My parents decided to do so. In the presence of the king, the nobility and the people, Master Vincent made a Sign of the Cross over me; after which I immediately resumed all the normal functions of life, and I have remained completely cured ever since. In my opinion I was possessed by an evil spirit who left my body with violence on the order of the Master Vincent."

.The master affirmed that during the whole of this time a good spirit had kept life and strength in the child in so far as to allow him to grow.

Vincent preached three times before the English king and his court, and a large number of people of different nationalities. Yet each one of these understood all he said as though he were speaking the idiom of their own language with the utmost clarity and a thoroughly comprehensive grasp of its meaning.

The political outcome of this visit was the signing of a three years truce which gave France breathing space in which to prepare for her salvation later on by the hands of Joan of Arc.

# Chapter XXII

## Precious in the Sight of the Lord
## Is the Death of His Saints

Early in 1419, Vincent Ferrer returned to Vannes to
die. His second entry into that city was as magnificent as
his first had been. Again the duchess sent her litter, and
this time through deference and a gracious desire to show
gratitude, it was not refused. The same sentiment of
grateful recognition induced him to accept the hospitality
of a nobleman named Dreulin, a close friend of the duke
and duchess.

Each day he sang Mass and preached, and for miles
round people flocked to hear him. Until his death agony
came on him, the apostle preserved his courage, his memory,
his strength of will and the austerity of his life. He had
grown so feeble that before and after preaching he was
unable to walk alone; only his marvellous voice, and the
wonderful mind which directed it were still vital and
youthful. Every day of this last Lent he preached; he was
to die before its end.

The care which his kind hosts lavished on him was
abundantly repaid in his own fashion. One of the chil-

dren of the house, with a child's predeliction for mischief, playing near a pan of boiling water, fell in. Vincent made the Sign of the Cross over the blistered body and the little one was immediately completely cured.

For a time his hosts moved him to a little village just outside called Roscoff, an enchanted spot beside the sea, where the air is soft and sweet, and where the trees and flowers are as beautiful and grow in the same profusion as they do in the master's native Spain. There the dying apostle refreshed his soul in those beauties of sky and sea which had always meant so much to him. From time immemorial the owners of the villa where he stayed have preserved in an oaken chest a stone, an object of veneration, known as the pillow of Saint Vincent Ferrer.

Full of grief at the thought of losing their beloved master, protector and brother, and still more distressed at the thought that his glorious tomb would be far from his and their own country, the Valencians of his following renewed their supplications that Vincent should come home with them to die. Death was to the master so completely a home-coming that those round him had no embarrassment in speaking of it before him. Smiling, the apostle acquiesced for the second time, and made his preparations to depart.

He bade farewell to the duchess and her court, and they, though deeply grieved at losing him, made no effort to stay his departure. After all, no one loves his native land better than the Breton, and so they quite understood the feeling which animated the Spaniards.

As for his followers, from their point of view, they were in charge of a great treasure, not their own but held in trust for their country. Without Vincent they knew they would be ill-received in Valencia; besides, as a matter of justice and propriety, it was fitting that the land which gave him birth should also guard his remains.

"Spain, your own Spain, wants you, has need of you," they told Vincent. "If you are going to be ill, where can you have greater hope of your recovery than in your native air? If you are to die it is only fitting that you should be buried in Spain."

But since they knew that it would be easier to carry off the whole town of Vannes itself than Vincent out of the town, they decided to leave by night, and, in fact, under cover of darkness they actually set out. They carried him down to the waiting ship, but no sooner had he embarked than Vincent's malady was so suddenly and unexpectedly aggravated that they were obliged to put back again to port.

When, with the morning, he returned to Vannes, the church bells rang, a general holiday was proclaimed, and with great rejoicing the folk hurried to meet him.

For the last time he blessed and cured all the sick who presented themselves, and then he spoke to all: "Go now, my children. God has sent me back, not to preach any more to you, but to die. Go back to your houses and God will reward you for the honors which your love has deemed it right to shew me."

That evening he was taken with a violent fever accompanied by an extremely sharp pain, but in spite of all the smile never left his face. Some of those around him, with little thought for the feelings of the dying man, begged him to settle a dispute which had arisen between the townsfolk and his own Order respecting his burial place.

"I am nothing more than a poor friar, the servant of Jesus Christ," answered Vincent. "And so I am much more engaged with the matter of my soul's salvation, than with what becomes of my body after death. So do not let it be-

225

come the cause of dispute or disturbance. The prior of the nearest Convent of Friars Preachers should be allowed to have the disposal of such matters."

The nobles of the court of Brittany, the magistrates of the town, the commonality, all came in turn to visit him and all wept inconsolably. Vincent comforted them as best he could.

*Talk to the Bretons, before his death at Vannes.* "Messires, Bretons," he said, "if you guard in your memory all that I have preached to you during these past two years, you will find that it is as useful as it is comformable with truth. You are not ignorant that there are certain vices to which this province is subject. And you know that I have neglected nothing in order to bring you back to the right path. Give thanks to God with me that after He has given me the gift of preaching the word, He has likewise given fruit to that preaching by rendering your hearts capable of being touched and led in the right path. Now it only remains for you to persevere in the practice of virtue; nor must you forget what you have learnt from me. As for myself, since it has pleased God that I should find here an end of my labors, I will be your advocate before the tribunal of God, and I will not cease to implore His mercy on you. This I promise you on condition that you in no way depart from what I have taught you. Now, good-bye. In ten days time I shall appear before my Lord."

Afterwards he spoke alone with his disciples, pouring out his heart to them as their apostle, their brother, and their friend. When at last he was left to himself, he asked one of the priests in attendance to give him the Absolution and Indulgence *in articulo mortis,* which was the only favor that he would accept from Pope Martin V when that Pontiff asked him what reward he desired in recompense for the many services which he had rendered to the Church.

After this he received the Last Sacraments. "In this," says his biographer, "he acted like the rest of men, so that when pale Death came she would not hesitate to claim him, thinking him no true man, but a heavenly spirit hidden in a human form."

After he had received all the Last Rites of the Church, his soul rested united to its Creator in a sweet and serene ecstasy. But there was no serenity among the inconsolable people outside the sick-room, and they begged to be allowed to see him and receive his blessing again for the last time. Willingly, in spite of the mortal weakness which possessed him, he agreed to their request. And so the whole town came once more to his bedside and his hand of benediction rested on the head of each one of them.

On the ninth day, the livid pallor of his face announced to those watching him the approach of death. The master asked for the Passion according to the four Evangelists to be read aloud to him, followed by the seven penitential psalms, after which he himself said the entire psalter by heart. In these, his last moments, this just man experienced extraordinary sentiments of repentance. The bystanders were distressed to see the shrinking of his whole person and the beads of sweat which stood out on his forehead as he repeated the verses of the psalms which spoke of sin and sorrow for sin.

They said to him: "Beloved master, we can do nothing for you but repeat the counsels which you have so often given others: have confidence in God and His mercy."

At this Vincent raised his hands and eyes to heaven with an expression of the utmost confidence.

The people now started the prayers for the dying, and as they ended the invocations to the saints for this saint who was now going to become one of that glorious army, he joined his hands, raised his eyes to heaven and for the last time kissed his Crucifix. Then his face lit up with joy, and so he peacefully ended his earthly pilgrimage.

He died on the Wednesday in Passion week, April 5th.

The duchess of Brittany, who was present at his death, herself claimed the privilege of washing the master's feet. "How beautiful are the feet of those who preach peace, the Good News!" Then his followers straightway barricaded the house, because rumors were going round the town that the Franciscans, or his brother Dominicans, were intending to take the body away, and both they and the townsfolk were determined that it should not leave Vannes.

Those in the death chamber were the witnesses of a beautiful happening. No sooner was the master dead than a multitude of butterflies of shining whiteness flew through the open window into the room, drawn as we may believe by the exquisite perfume which exhaled from the body of the saint. These small butterflies, according to a contemporary account, seemed to dance in the air, as though with their little wings they wished to make music to sing the triumph of Vincent's entry into heaven.

The archbishop and chapter caused the holy remains to be guarded with the utmost care, and that same evening they were carried to the cathedral, to lie in state in the choir. The concourse of people who came to venerate the master's body was so great that the authorities were obliged to leave it unburied until Friday, guarded all the time by soldiers. During the whole of this time it preserved its suppleness; the color had not left the face which was full of serenity and repose. There it lay in its full perfection and the perfume which filled the church was even perceptible outside.

It was buried between the choir and the High Altar, on the north side, in front of the episcopal chair, on Friday, April 7th, at four o'clock in the afternoon.

Let Saint Vincent himself have the last word in this book. It is taken from a sermon preached on the Tuesday after the feast of Pentecost, on the text: "I have come that they may have life, and may have it more abundantly" (John: 10.10).

"The third kind of life which we owe to the Holy Spirit is the celestial life. This is the difference between human and animal souls, for the soul of a brute beast is not a subsisting, spiritual and incorruptible substance, it is substantial form immersed in matter, which has no being without matter and body. It has its whole being in its body, since it has been brought into actuality from matter in potency; and because, as we have already said, it has its whole being in body, therefore, when the body is destroyed, the whole corrupts. *From the sermons; given on the Tuesday after Pentacost; on celestial and eternal life.*

"But the soul of man is a spiritual substance like the angels, and receives nothing from the body, but itself gives being and life to the body. Therefore, when the body fails it still remains. . . . So, it follows that if the soul of a man orders itself well, the body is rewarded, just like the soldier who guards well the fortress which has been entrusted to him by the king. When God creates the soul, at its creation He pours it into the fortress of the body, that it may rule it according to God's will, so that the enemy may not enter by the gates of the senses. If therefore it governs it well it is rewarded, if badly it is punished.

"When, therefore, a soul which has ruled well the fortress

229

of its body leaves that body by death, it comes immediately before Christ, saying: 'Lord, I have kept the fortress which Thou hast given me.' And Christ will give it celestial life in heaven. As we read in the Epistle to the Romans (8.11): 'If Christ be in you—that is, by grace and a good life—the body indeed is dead because of sin; but the spirit liveth because of justification. And if the Spirit of him that raised up Jesus Christ from the dead dwell in you, he that raised up Jesus Christ from the dead shall quicken also your mortal bodies because of his Spirit that dwelleth in you.'

"But you may say: 'From whom do we get this celestial life?' I answer that this celestial life is appropriated to the Holy Spirit. Like the mist, which rises from the earth in the morning and is drawn up by the heat of the sun causing it to rise, so the soul cannot ascend to heaven, unless it is drawn up by the informing, indwelling heat of the Holy Spirit. So says David: 'Thou hast made me to live in justice.' I assure you, in consequence, that this life is most exceedingly to be desired. It is as if a powerful Lord in his will were to leave you a high, impregnable fortress, of which you had not as yet taken possession; O how you would long for it! Your desire for heaven, that impregnable fortress above, should be more vehement still. Therefore Christ says: 'To him that thirsteth—that is ardently longs for—I will give of the fountain of the water of life freely. He that shall overcome shall possess these things. And I will be his God and he shall be My son. But the fearful and the unbelieving and the abominable and murderers and whoremongers and sorcerers and idolaters and all liars, they shall have their portion in the pool burning with fire and brimstone which is the second death. And there came one of the seven angels, who had the vials full of the seven last plagues, and spoke with me saying:

230

'Come and I will shew thee the bride, the wife of the Lamb.' Notice how this whole chapter speaks of the exceeding beauty of the Kingdom.

"The fourth life is Eternal Life, that is when, at the day of Judgment we shall all rise, both body and soul. The good shall rise with glorified bodies, and with these bodies they will live eternally. If you ask: 'And is not the life of the souls of the saints as they now dwell in heaven eternal?' I answer, 'No,' which is true in respect to this mode of being, because now the souls of the saints are separated from their bodies; but at the Judgment and General Resurrection they will be reunited to these bodies in glory. . . . God will reward every one according to the life he has lived here and the good works he has performed. Now in the good acts which we perform here, there is this order: the first movement is in the soul only, by thought, deliberation, and ordination, and so the soul is the first to merit. Then, in the carrying out of the work, the body takes its part. Therefore, the soul is the first to be rewarded, then the body, at the Last Judgment. . .

"This eternal life is appropriated to the Holy Spirit, because by nature our spirit goes forth and does not return; but by the power of the Holy Spirit dwelling in the soul, each soul dons again its own proper body. And this is not difficult to the Holy Spirit, for He who created all things out of nothing, can easily unite body and soul in one. 'And if the Spirit of him that raised up Jesus Christ from the dead dwell in you, he that raised up Jesus Christ from the dead shall quicken also your mortal bodies, because of his Spirit that dwelleth in you.'

"This life is to be looked for with the greatest certitude. . . . Jesus Christ has said: 'Wonder not at this: for the hour cometh, wherein all that are in the graves shall hear

231

the voice of the Son of God. And they that have done good things shall come forth into the resurrection of life; but they that have done evil unto the resurrection of judgment.' Wonder not at this, the resurrection, for to God nothing is difficult, because the hour cometh, the judgment, wherein all that are in the graves shall hear the voice of the Son of God: that is when He commands: 'Arise ye dead and come to judgment.'

"Therefore it can be seen how we have four lives from the Holy Spirit: corporal, spiritual, celestial, and eternal. That is why He says: 'Behold I have come that they may have life': that is spiritual, celestial and eternal, which may the Glorious Spirit give to us. Thanks be to God."

# INDEX:

The following sermons, prayers and letters of Vincent Ferrer are incorporated into the text and marked throughout by marginal notes.

Preacher and prophet, Saint Vincent Ferrer lived from 1350 to 1419 and roamed Western Europe for twenty years at the end of his life as an Ambassador of Christ. On foot, or upon a donkey, preaching for as long as six hours at a time, and followed by an army of as many as 10,000 disciples, he travelled in Spain and France, Italy, the Alpine countries and south Germany.

He converted thousands of Jews and Moors, brought other thousands of lapsed Christians back to the Church, and was instrumental in ending the great schism that saw one Pope at Rome and another at Avignon. One of his contemporaries has said of him: "Every step was a miracle, every word a victory for heaven."

Kings, princes and bishops, as well as the multitude of the faithful, sought his advice and time and again he confirmed